W9-DDH-266

ARCHAEOLOGY OF INDUSTRY

The Archaeology of Industry

KENNETH HUDSON

Drawings by
PIPPA BRAND

CHARLES SCRIBNER'S SONS · New York

FRONTISPIECE
The Great Pit at the
copper mine, Falun,
Sweden, in the late
eighteenth century.

Copyright © 1976 Kenneth Hudson
Drawings Copyright © 1976 The Bodley Head

Copyright under the Berne Convention

All rights reserved. No part of this book
may be reproduced in any form without the
permission of Charles Scribner's Sons.

1 3 5 7 9 11 13 15 17 19 I/C 20 18 16 14 12 10 8 6 4 2

Printed in Great Britain
Library of Congress Catalog Card Number 75-38404
ISBN 0-684-14592-8

CONTENTS

ACKNOWLEDGMENTS

Among the many people around the world who have helped me, both in forming my ideas and in obtaining information, I should like to thank especially: Georges van den Abeelen (Belgium); Neil Cossons (UK); Eric DeLony (United States); Marcel Evrard (France); Frank Hawtin (UK); Anders Jespersen (Denmark); Werner Kroker (West Germany); Robert Legget (Canada); Marie Nisser (Sweden); Arthur Percival (UK); Paul Stumes (Canada); Ray Sutcliffe (UK); Hugues de Varine-Bohan (France); Robert M. Vogel (United States); Otfried Wagenbreth (East Germany) and Cyril Walmsley (UK).

Thanks are due to the following for permission to reproduce black-and-white photographs: Stora Kopparberg, Falun, Sweden, frontispiece and page 30; Frank Hawtin, page 10; Charles Léva, page 16; Bath and Portland Stone Group, pages 21 and 23; Bodie State Historic Park, California, page 26; Ann Nicholls, page 33; Museum of Man and Industry, Le Creusot, pages 36, 39, 40; Allaire State Park, New Jersey, page 47; Crofton Society of the Kennet and Avon Canal Trust, pages 50 and 51; Faversham Society, pages 55 and 57; the Hagley Property Museum, Delaware, pages 58 and 60; Simon van der Stel Foundation, Pretoria, page 65; Gelardin, Bruner, Cott, Inc, Cambridge, Massachusetts, page 69; Anders Jespersen, pages 71 and 72; Borough of Thamesdown, page 76; the Trustees of the British Museum, page 79; James Austin, page 81; W. A. McCutcheon, page 83; the Guildhall Library, London, page 85; French Railways, page 89; Deutsche Fotothek, Dresden, page 90; the Smithsonian Institution, Washington, DC, page 92; Eric de Maré, page 95; Robert F. Legget, page 98; Mystic Seaport, Connecticut, page 102; Taylor Woodrow Property Company Ltd, London, page 104; Lufthansa, page 107; British Aircraft Corporation, page 108; Chicago Historical Society, page 111; Carlsberg, Copenhagen, page 117; Champagne Museum, Épernay, France, page 120; Courtauld Institute of Art, page 122.

For permission to use coloured photographs thanks are due to: the Ironbridge Gorge Museum Trust, jacket; Sovereign Hill, Ballarat, Victoria, facing page 32 (*above*); Ann Nicholls, facing page 32 (*below*), facing pages 48 and 49, facing page 97 (*above* and *below*), facing page 112; John Maggs, Falmouth, facing page 33 (*above*) The Metal Society, London, facing page 33 (*below*); the Science Museum, London, facing page 96, facing page 113 (*above*); the London Museum, facing page 113 (*below*).

Thanks are also due to William Collins Sons for permission to quote from *I Know My Love* by Catherine Gaskin on pages 24–5.

The publishers have made every effort to trace the owners of copyright material appearing in this book. In the event of any question arising as to the use of such material, the publishers, while expressing regret for any error unconsciously made, will be pleased to make the necessary correction in any future edition.

INTRODUCTION

This book is concerned mainly with the period from 1750 onwards and with what nowadays is often called 'industrial archaeology', a portmanteau term for the surviving evidence of yesterday's ways of making and selling things, and of moving goods and people from one place to another. This evidence may, as with old railway stations, canals, textile mills or quarries, be readily visible, or it may, like the sites of former potteries, glassworks and ironworks, only reveal itself after decades of rubbish have been cleared from the ruins of collapsed and abandoned buildings. Sometimes the old machinery will still be there, but more often it will have disappeared, leaving only the shell of a former mill or engine-house to remind us of the work that was once carried on there. Not infrequently the machinery, or part of it, has been installed in a museum while the building that housed it has been demolished or converted to other purposes.

Strictly speaking, what has been transferred to museums is not archaeology. It is preferable, but not always possible, to reserve that word for what still remains on the original site. But no archaeologist, industrial or otherwise, will confine his attention to archaeology. His business is to use what he finds on the site as a means of improving his understanding of a particular period, industry or technology, and he will naturally want to incorporate this special knowledge with the other information which already exists. One kind of evidence supports and enriches another. A derelict and empty cotton mill, for instance, can give a good idea of the size of the enterprise and of the techniques used to construct a building which had to be reasonably fireproof, provide adequate natural light, accommodate a large number of people and a great deal of heavy equipment, and withstand the pounding and vibration of the steam-engine and machinery. Such a building can only be brought alive, however, and put into a meaningful human and industrial context by talking to retired workers, looking at looms and spinning machines in museums, visiting a functioning cotton mill to hear and see what the processes involve, searching for old photographs and sifting through a wide range of printed and manuscript material—catalogues, histories of the cotton industry and of individual firms within it, memoirs, letters, newspapers.

No one kind of evidence provides the complete picture, and even with all the available information to hand, a lively imagination is needed to make sense of it. It is the questions we ask no less than the answers we receive which allow us to develop a feeling for the past, without which the most painstaking and academically respectable research is pointless and a waste of time. Was this cotton mill heated in the winter? How was it heated? If there was no heating, how did the operatives manage to do their work? What kind of sanitary facilities were provided? Where were they situated? What sort of food and drink did Victorian mill-hands bring with them to work? Where did they eat it? What were the most common kinds of accident? And since weaving was a very noisy occupation, did it make the weavers deaf?

Answers to all these questions must exist somewhere, but it is remarkable how the existing histories of the industry ignore them. The great value of industrial archaeology is that it has brought into the historical field a large number of practical-minded people with a taste for awkward questions. They want to know things which the traditional, library-bound historians never thought interesting or important, and to them it seems ridiculous to divide history into compartments—political history, economic history, social history, the history of science and technology, and so on. There is just history, and industrial archaeology can be as helpful to the person whose main interest is machinery or steam-engines as to the student of disease or revolution. History is primarily about people, not things, and industrial archaeology, as one of the historian's tools, is about the part that coal-mines, steam-hammers and abandoned airship hangars played in the lives and thinking of the people who designed and operated them.

In this book we shall be looking at sites which have involved excavation and at sites where all the surviving evidence is to be found above ground; at sites which have been abandoned to their fate and at sites which have been restored and preserved; at buildings which are now nothing more than empty husks and at buildings which still have their original machinery and equipment in them. We are interested in factories and mills that have been converted into offices or flats, in old railway stations that are now garages, and in the housing that industrial firms have built for their workers at different periods. All this represents the archaeology of industry and transport.

1

Mining and Quarrying

One day, no doubt, there will be some form of scientific equipment which will make it possible for us to stand on the surface and look straight down through the soil and the rock at old mine-workings several hundred feet below. When that happens, it will be fascinating to see with our own eyes how impossibly narrow and low-roofed the nineteenth-century galleries were, and what a maze of criss-crossing tunnels they often form. At the moment, however, we are restricted to drawings and plans for our information about early coal and metal mining, reinforced by contemporary descriptions and by cut-away models in museums. For later periods, there are photographs and films to help us, and a number of technical museums, such as those in Prague, Bochum, Vienna and Munich, have mock-ups of coal-mines in their basements, to give visitors a fairly realistic impression of equipment and working conditions below ground. (One is unfortunately bound to say 'fairly realistic', because no museum has yet thought fit to fill its visitors' lungs with coal-dust, or to arrange for explosions of gas or inrushes of water from time to time, in order to show what conditions were really like.) Occasionally, as at the old demonstration silver-mine at Freiberg, in Germany, or at the modern silver-mine at Falun, in Sweden, members of the public are taken on conducted tours of parts of the workings, which certainly helps to bring the pictures and models to life. One of the most enterprising attempts to show the development of mining methods is at the Slovak mining museum at Banská Stiavnica in Czechoslovakia. Under the museum building runs a gallery where miners worked silver in the first half of the eighteenth century. This has been made into an underground museum 76·2 metres long,

Boys and girls from Backwell School excavating a flue at the lead works at Charterhouse-on-Mendip.

where visitors can see the various types of framing and timbering used in ore-mining, shaft winding installations and other examples of mining techniques.

For the most part, however, the archaeology of mining is above ground and the old buildings usually disappear quickly once the mine goes out of use or is transformed in the course of a modernisation programme. In such cases, all that is likely to survive of previous operations is a waste-tip or two, and nowadays even these tend to be carted away for road-material or for levelling building sites. But even waste-tips and holes in the ground can provide useful information if they are studied with method and imagination as Frank Hawtin, of the Somerset County Museum, has shown during his investigations in the historic lead-mining area at Charterhouse-on-Mendip. He carried them out with the help of school parties attending courses at the County's field studies centre at Charterhouse and with the help of a torrential rainstorm in 1968 which did much of the excavation work for them. This storm obligingly revealed the foundations of buildings where a works was established in 1855 to extract silver from the local silver-lead ore which had been worked since Roman times.

Archaeological investigation of the site showed the remains of a furnace and chimney and a stone-lined flue, a great deal of soot and a glazed fire-brick (evidence of the intense heat that the process required). Several lead slugs, 19 mm in diameter, were also found, which fitted into assay-moulds lying on another part of the site. One of these lead samples contained, on analysis, 0·39 per cent of silver and, since the process then in use could reduce the silver content much lower than this, the archaeologists made the reasonable deduction that the sample had been taken at a midway stage in the extraction process.

In a heap of rubble there was a broken ginger-beer bottle, bearing two inscriptions—one 'Redfern Bros. Bottle Makers, Barnsley', and 'Ball and Pinnel (Bristol)', the producers of the ginger-beer. An enquiry to Redfern Bros., who were still in business, elicited the fact that the date of the bottle was about 1890, at which time the works is known to have been in full operation. The fact that the bottle contained ginger-beer, not beer, is interesting. At this time bottled beer was rather flat and of a far from uniform quality. Ginger-beer was altogether more exciting. Working men preferred draught beer when they could get it, but on this remote Mendip site supplies were not likely to be easy to get and something more easily portable no doubt had its attractions. Other identifiable objects included pieces of fire-brick stamped with the maker's name, 'Rufford' and the place of manufacture, 'Stourbridge'.

The archaeological techniques used here were identical with those which would have been used on any non-industrial site. The excavation, plans of the foundations, identification of signed bottles and bricks, analysis of metal-samples and so on are all normal practice when obtaining and recording information at the kind of places with which classical and medieval archaeologists are familiar. Charterhouse-on-Mendip is different in two important respects, however. The first is that the archaeology fits into a pattern of in-formation which already exists. J. W. Gough's standard work, *The Mines of Mendip* (1930, reissued by David & Charles, 1967), tells the story of these mines and we do not have to guess at the techniques, the operators and the dates. And the second difference is that there are still family memories and family records of the people who

Dortmund-Böving-hausen. Store and other buildings (1901) at the pit.

worked there. The human story of the mines is not too difficult to piece together, at least for the second half of the nineteenth century.

Fashions in the writing of history change, however. Today we are interested in things which appear to have mattered very little to historians of Gough's generation. We like to know how much miners earned, what their living and working conditions were like, what kind of accidents they had to face, what happened to them when they were ill or unemployed, and so on. We are not content merely with accounts of processes, quantities and prices.

Charterhouse-on-Mendip represents the archaeology of mining at its most basic, with no buildings standing and the surviving machinery and equipment reduced to three or four fire-bars. On other sites there is a great deal more to see. One of the most spectacular is the remarkable mining complex at Dortmund-Böving-hausen in Germany, which dates from the early years of the present century. Most of it is still intact, although it is no longer in use. One approaches the mine through a pleasant garden-city estate, goes

The Art Nouveau
entrance to the
Machinery Hall,
Dortmund-Böving-
hausen.

through the entrance gates, and is immediately faced with what
looks remarkably like the courtyard of a large and well endowed
English public school, with lawns, trees and brick buildings in an
Art Nouveau style, with very little suggestion of industry about
them. They are, in fact, the former pit-head baths and administration block of the mine, now leased to a number of other manufacturing and commercial concerns.

Having crossed this courtyard, one is to some extent prepared for
the huge Machinery Hall, which is linked up to it. This splendid
structure, also Art Nouveau, was designed in 1901 by the celebrated
German architect, Bruno Möhring. It was built to house the mine's
power plant and electric winding gear and its splendours include
stained glass and marble control panels, as well as the original
Siemens dynamos and associated equipment, the first to be installed
in a German coal-mine. The walls of the engineers' rest room are
generously papered with pin-ups from both World Wars and the
whole hall looks, if not exactly like Pompeii before it was covered

13

with volcanic lava, much as though the day shift had just left and the night shift not yet arrived.

The mine closed down in the 1950s. The shaft has been covered over and the installations above it demolished and cleared away. There are no waste-heaps nearby, and apart from the railway yard where pit-props used to be unloaded and stacked there is very little else to recall the days when this was one of the biggest and most productive mines in the Ruhr. The whole site now belongs to the Mining Museum at Bochum, which plans progressively to get rid of the present tenants of the buildings and to establish a museum of the industries of the Ruhr there.

What information do these buildings give us that we would be unlikely to get in any other way? What do they add to the historical record? The best way of answering this is to put another question. Why did the owners of the mine decide to spend so much more money than they needed to have done? So far as we can judge, there were two main reasons. They wanted to go one better than the other coal owners, partly, no doubt, for reasons of vanity ('We have employed the most prestigious architect available and given him his head') but partly, also, because they believed that above-average buildings would make for greater efficiency. A wish to look after the welfare of the company's employees was certainly an important factor—the housing estate, the lawns, the apprentice-school with its gymnasium, and the splendid bath-building are there to prove it. Even the mortuary is Art Nouveau. But, in the climate of opinion which prevailed in German industry at the beginning of the century, efficiency, snobbery, patriotism and attention to welfare were inseparable. These mine installations at Dortmund represent the paternalistic German employer doing his very best for the nation, for the coal industry, for his workers and, hardly incidentally, for himself. A walk round the site tells us a great deal about German morale and ambitions during the years before the First World War, more, perhaps, than we are likely to get from a considerable amount of reading of political history. What remains of this great mine, its archaeology, expresses the many-sided strength of German industry at its pre-war peak—and one or two of its weaknesses.

We can explore coal-mining from a rather different angle at Le Grand-Hornu, near Mons, in Belgium. This is the area known as the Borinage, immortalised by Emile Zola in his novel, *Germinal*, as one of the poorest, most brutal and most harshly exploited parts of industrial Europe during the nineteenth century. Yet in the 1820s

Child miners in the
Borinage about 1900.

and 1830s, one of the most important and enlightened of the coal owners in Belgium was a man called Henri de Gorge-Legrand. He used up-to-date techniques, with a steam-engine to power the machinery in his workshops, a horse-drawn railway—the first in Belgium—to link his pits with the Mons Canal, and a town for his work-people which had amenities that were remarkable for the time. There was a school, a community centre and reading room, public baths and a dance hall. The main square contained a band-stand, where the town band gave concerts twice a week during the summer months. These buildings are still to be seen, although, with the disappearance of the coal industry from the district, most of them have been considerably modernised and adapted by their new owners.

The most impressive of Henri de Gorge-Legrand's creations was, and still is, the vast elliptical courtyard which contained the assembly shops, foundries, stores and administration block of the business which made and repaired all kinds of machinery, including loco-motives, for the Legrand pits, and for those belonging to other

15

Inner courtyard at Le Grand-Hornu in the days of its prosperity. Based on a contemporary print.

Aerial view of Le Grand-Hornu, showing former workshops, workers' houses, and towards the right, the owners' château.

companies. A noted French architect, Bruno Renard, was employed, and he produced an excellently proportioned group of buildings, which gave, as Legrand wanted, prestige and grandeur to a functional building. Few alterations were made to the buildings during the period of more than a century when they were in continuous use, until coal-mining in the area came to an end in 1951. One distinguished addition was a cast-iron statue of Henri de Gorge-Legrand, which still stands in the middle of the courtyard. It was erected in his memory in 1855.

After 1951 the buildings ceased to be maintained and began to decay rapidly. Roofs fell in, pillars collapsed, plants began to grow in the ruins and by the mid-sixties Bruno Renard's masterpiece appeared more than ripe for the demolition contractors—all the more when a Royal decree was published that ordered the complete removal of all traces of the former coal industry in the Borinage, partly on aesthetic grounds but even more to obliterate the district's *Germinal*-type associations. At this point a successful architect, Henri Guchez, who had been born and brought up in Le Grand-Hornu, offered to buy the entire site from the Government, which by this time had become the owners. After much difficulty, and a fair amount of ridicule, he was allowed to buy it, and since then he has spent a fortune in restoring and modernising the premises, and in installing his own large architectural practice there, so that buildings which once accommodated fitters and machine operators are now filled with decorous rows of drawing-boards and draughtsmen. The

17

A woman with coal picked from a waste-tip in the Borinage. Based on an artist's drawing, 1889.

courtyard is to be a lake, with water-lilies and swans and the statue of Henri de Gorge-Legrand rising from the middle of the water. The former stable block in the outer courtyard has been transformed into an exhibition centre and, facing it, an old sugar factory is being restored in preparation for its future use as a museum of industry and technology. Despite the Royal decree, the project on which Renard and his patron lavished so much care and money has been saved for posterity.

The workers' *cité*, too, seems safe, and its terraced houses—there are more than four hundred of them—show the standard which an exceptionally progressive employer of the 1820s thought appropriate. Each house has three rooms downstairs and three upstairs, together with a cellar. Each house has a garden and a coal-house, for the waste coal which was supplied cheaply by the company. There was a well and an oven for every ten houses. Some of the houses still have their original wooden shutters and in one or two the old stable-type doors have been preserved.

The houses were rented by the week, and the company's records show that they were inhabited by families of between six and ten people, with often a lodger as well. The father, mother and older children worked either in the mine or in the workshops, and the company had the right to possession of the house if a man was dismissed. This probably discouraged strikes and political activity, but there were certainly compensations in working at Le Grand Hornu. Some of them have already been mentioned, but there was also the advantage of a butcher's shop, a bakery, and a general store which was reckoned to sell better quality goods at lower prices.

What was achieved at Le Grand Hornu cannot be properly valued or understood without knowing something of the conditions which other workers in the area had to tolerate during the first half of the nineteenth century. The miserable hovels in which a large proportion of them lived fortunately engaged the attention of a number of contemporary writers and artists. Vincent Van Gogh, who spent a period in the Borinage as an independent missionary, was one of them. If we, with our present-day interest in social and industrial history, had been unable to see what Henri de Gorge-Legrand did, if all his buildings had been demolished during the 1950s and '60s, as they could well have been, the picture of coal-mining in the Borinage might have been one of unrelieved poverty, squalor and general beastliness. The archaeology allows us to correct this impression, to set the record straight, and to realise that it was possible for an industrialist of this period to have ideals of fair treatment and of dignified, even beautiful surroundings, which might come as a considerable surprise to anyone who relied entirely on written or painted sources for his information.

The archaeology of stone quarrying is of two types, the quarries themselves and the buildings which were constructed with the stone. The first offers clues as to how the stone was extracted, and the second tells us about the way it was used, and about its wearing qualities. The underground quarries near Corsham, in Wiltshire, together with the houses, walls and bridges in the surrounding towns and villages, give us good examples of both kinds of archaeology.

Since Roman times the area around Bath has provided limestone which could be quarried in large blocks and which could be easily cut and carved. Georgian Bath was built for the most part of stone found in the immediate vicinity, but the construction of Box Tunnel, a few miles to the east of Bath, between 1838 and 1841, as part of Brunel's Great Western Railway from Bristol to London, revealed enormous deposits of good quality stone and encouraged the development of mining, rather than quarrying. Mining was not new in the Box and Corsham district—stone was being mined at Corsham as early as 1770—but the early technique was to get at the stone by means of short tunnels or adits driven straight into the side of the hill. Most of the traces of adit-mining have now been obliterated, and so, very recently, has the most impressive example of what was known as vertical shaft entry. This particular mine, in Box Fields, was known as 'The Cathedral'. It was worked from 1830 to 1850 by the old method that was in use before the introduction of the saw— the stone was chiselled out by means of hammers and wedges and a long iron bar called a 'yad'. 'The Cathedral' was worked downwards, and galleries were driven off at three levels to find the good stone. The quarried stone was then pulled up to the surface, through a hole in the roof. When the Great Western Railway was built the demand for Box-Corsham stone greatly increased, and by 1862 there were more than eight kilometres of tunnels in the area, with horse-drawn and gravity tramways to haul the stone from the face and up a sloping shaft to the surface. In 1904, when nearly 2,830 cubic metres of stone were being produced each year, it was claimed that there were over 96 kilometres of underground roadway in the Wiltshire stone mines. It was possible to walk direct from Clift Quarry, Box, to Tunnel Quarry, Corsham, a distance of about five kilometres, in a straight line.

Wooden pit-props were sometimes used in these workings, but the usual method was to leave wide pillars of stone uncut, to support the roof. The freestone beds, which are from six to nine metres thick, lie mostly at about sixty metres from the surface. Air shafts have been dug at various points, but no form of mechanically aided ventilation is needed. The temperature and atmosphere in the mines are very agreeable at all times of the year.

The technique of mining the stone changed very little until after the Second World War. The men used a series of picks with handles of different lengths to chip out a slot, known as the picking-bed, about 250 mm thick and 1·5 to 1·8 metres deep immediately below the roof. This was a slow and laborious job. The stone was worked in steps, so that it was possible to stand on the block immediately below the one that was being quarried. A saw was put into the gap that had been picked out, and the stone was sawn into blocks downwards to the natural division between the layers of the bed. Levers were driven in horizontally at this point, and the block was split away from the mass, eased out of the bed with the help of a crane and lowered on to the floor of the mine.

Nowadays the mines are electrically lit, and this allows one to see thousands of small round black patches dotting the roof. These are soot deposits from the tiny oil-lamps used by the miners while they were picking and sawing the stone, and a permanent reminder of the semi-darkness in which the job used to be done. In places one can see old saw-sharpening files hammered into the stone at intervals to hang a light on; sometimes a little niche was cut in a pillar for the same purpose.

Once the block was free from the bed, it was possible to discover, by tapping it with an iron bar, if it contained a flaw or crack. If it did, the quarryman knocked off small pieces of stone until he came to the source of the trouble. The block was then lifted on to a trolley and taken to the surface. At Monks Park mine, the only one still in operation, the stone contained a good deal of moisture, so that blocks quarried during the winter had to remain underground until the spring, when all danger of frost, which would have split the 'green' block, had passed. At Box Hill, on the other hand, the stone could be brought to the surface straight away.

In the older parts of the workings at Monks Park one can see shallow holes in the roof, about 25 mm square and about 50 mm deep. The cranes fitted into these holes. They were very simple, hand-cranked affairs, made of two stout timbers, one upright and

OPPOSITE
The entrance to Monks Park underground quarry, Corsham.

20

the other, the lifting jib, swinging at an angle. The upright was slotted into the holes cut into the stone. As the face being worked moved forward, further holes were cut and the crane was dismantled and shifted forward to the new point. Abandoned cranes are still to be seen in the workings.

Once it had been brought to the surface, the stone was stacked up to 'cure' for twelve months or more until it was ready for sawing into blocks. Very little of it was wasted. The smaller pieces that were knocked off during operations at the mine were squared up to make usable facing or walling material, or sold as rubble which was mixed with mortar and used for interior walling, much as breezeblocks are today. If one takes a careful look at buildings in the Bath area, especially those under restoration, the thriftiness of the eighteenth- and nineteenth-century builders becomes apparent. The largest blocks were reserved for the façades of the more expensive and prestigious buildings, such as the great crescents in Bath and country mansions. Smaller blocks are to be found in cottages, the backs of the crescents, and garden walls. In this way, and by using rubble behind the dressed-stone fronts, the cost of the stone was kept low. Nowadays, when only the best stone can be marketed in its original form—much more is ground up and mixed with cement to make artificial or 'reconstituted' stone—the price is necessarily high.

Modern stone-mining is wasteful in another way. The old hand saws had narrow blades and very little stone was lost in the form of dust from the saw-cut. Since 1945, however, the stone at Monks Park has been cut mechanically, using coal-cutting machines of an ancient type long obsolete in the coal industry. These make a cut over 127 mm wide, so that many tons of good stone are inevitably and irretrievably lost each year during the process of getting the stone from the bed.

Monks Park mine is perhaps the most spectacular source of building stone in Britain, although the quarries on Portland would come a close second. But whether we are dealing with sites as huge as those at Portland and around Box and Corsham, or with much smaller local quarries, the question is always the same: how did our ancestors extract and move away such huge quantities of stone with such primitive equipment and with so few men? One answer is that, like the men who built the railways and bridges, they worked very long hours and took great risks. Accidents were frequent, and quarry accidents are likely to be serious. If one asks an old quarry-

Cutting blocks of stone for removal from the bed in the old way at Monks Park.

man about this, he will in all probability produce a series of harrowing tales of how this woman was left with five small children after her husband was crushed by a block of stone falling from a truck or a crane, how this relative lost a leg and how he himself was off work for months recovering from injuries caused by a runaway trolley. Such risks were accepted as part of the job. Between 1780 and 1850 the *Bath Chronicle* contains numerous news items, tucked away at the bottom of an inside page and rarely more than three or four lines long, reporting the death of a quarryman from an accident at work. Occurrences of this kind were so frequent that they hardly counted as news. But it is fair to point out that fatalities became much less frequent during the second half of the nineteenth century. Between 1883 and 1968 there were only fourteen known fatal accidents

23

underground—a tribute to the great care taken by the expert quarryman to test his ceilings.

The mines themselves contain many mementoes of the men who worked there. In places there are stone benches with a groove down the middle to hold a saw while it was being sharpened, and old files have been left where they were thrown down. The quarrymen made use of the pillars to work out their calculations of block sizes, and of the wages due to them. The pillars were also used as a kind of wall-newspaper, where the men recorded details of births, marriages and deaths and wrote up the dates of historical events, such as the beginning and end of the Crimean War. There are quotations from the Bible and from hymns, 'The Lord is my Shepherd' being particularly frequent. In complete contrast, there are attacks by one quarryman on another, often full of obscenities. Some of these pillar-writings refer to local matters, which no doubt meant a great deal at the time, but of which the point is now obscure.

The mines at Corsham are, perhaps, exceptional and dramatic examples of the archaeology of the stone industry, but other types of mining have caught the popular imagination for more than a century, long before the term 'industrial archaeology' began to be associated with such sites.

Ballarat in Australia, for instance, has a special place in both Australian and world history. It was a very ordinary sheep run in Victoria until it jumped into prominence in 1851 as the richest gold field that had ever been discovered. Thousands of immigrants poured into the Colony within a few years, as they were already doing in the American West, with the hope and intention of making a quick fortune. The usual type of gold-mining town came into existence at Ballarat, with its Main Street shops, dance halls, restaurants, hotels, grog shanties and theatres, allowing some people to spend a great deal of money and others to forget for a while that the gold had eluded them.

Ballarat has been a favourite subject for four generations of novelists. 'Here,' says the cover of one of the more recent, '30,000 men scramble for the gold under their feet by day—and every night drink it, gamble it away, or spend it on their women.' The actual picture, revealed in the pages of this same novel, was somewhat less exotic, with the women more likely to be found at work in the diggings than dressed up in the dance halls. 'All day,' one of them recalls, 'I watched the loads of dirt come up—I helped to wind the windlass to bring it to the surface. And then I took my turn with

Rose at rocking the cradle down the creek. The banks of the Yarrowee were lined on both sides with the wooden cradles and the valley was alive with the constant tumbling sound they made. One of us turned the handle and broke up the dirt with a stick, while the other kept water pouring on it. The deposit which fell through the wire sieves of the cradle had then to be washed in the tin pan for the dust. Con was deft at this. The quartz rock left in the cradle was picked over for pieces and lumps of gold. We found no lumps of gold. We got just enough from the dust Con panned to pay our daily expenses, and in this we were luckier than some.'

Ballarat was, unfairly, associated with violence, and this, too, has helped to keep the name alive. The diggers were for the most part an orderly body of men, but by 1854 their grievances against the authorities, especially over the method of granting licences, produced armed riots—the famous Eureka uprising—which were not easily forgotten.

Abandoned gold-workings are not very exciting places in themselves. Gold-rush mining consisted, for the most part, of digging small pits, working outwards from the bottom as far as was reasonably safe, hauling the earth and rock to the surface, and washing it to see if it contained any gold dust or, even better, nuggets. Once such an area is exhausted, the pits soon fill up, grass and bushes grow on the spoil heaps, and it takes a keen eye and a lively imagination to identify the places which were the scenes of so much frantic labour a century ago. This is as true of the British gold-workings, at, for example, Cilcain in Flintshire, as it is of Ballarat in Victoria, or Bodie in California.

The mining settlements themselves are another matter. The early buildings were usually made of wood, with stone or brick chimneys, and most of them have now either collapsed from decay or been burnt to ashes. At Ballarat, virtually none of the original buildings have survived, but a reconstructed settlement, known as Sovereign Hill, has been created close to the place where gold was first found. It provides, in the words of its sponsors, 'a realistic historical environment of the decade 1851–1861'. The exhibits illustrate the development of mining techniques from the early gold-panning days to the times when shafts were sunk hundreds of feet deep to reach the gold-bearing levels. There are underground mining scenes, and the huts and shanties of the diggers, complete with period furnishings. Many of the buildings of the old Main Street have been reconstructed, including some shops, the joss house, or temple, built by the Chinese

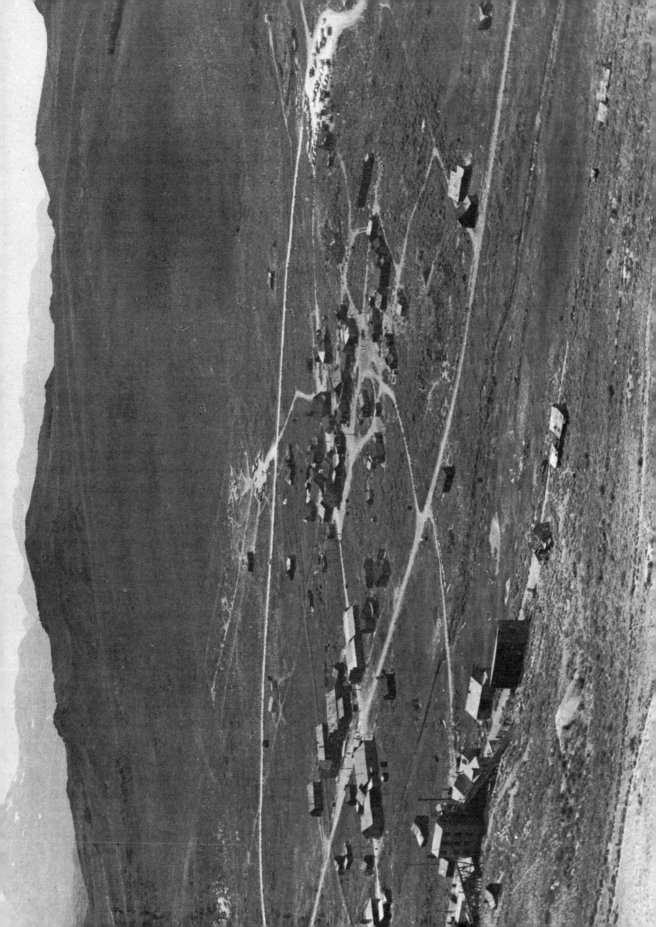

prospectors, and the *Ballarat Times* office, where there is a printer operating the antique press.

Sovereign Hill is what is nowadays known as a living history museum, an attempt to reconstruct the past and bring it alive. Another of the world's great gold-mining sites, at Bodie in California, is fortunate to have some original buildings, rather than reconstructions. But only about eighty—one in twenty—of the buildings the town contained in its heyday in 1880 still remain, and many of these are in a precarious condition: the California State Park System maintains Bodie in a state of what it calls 'arrested decay'.

The town had 10,000 people at its peak, and 65 saloons. Killings occurred with monotonous regularity, rarely fewer than one a day, and the fire-bell tolled the age of each victim as he was buried. The winter climate was, and is, vile, with snow six metres deep, winds of up to 160 kilometres an hour, and temperatures of forty degrees below zero. In conditions like these, perhaps the most important of the surviving buildings was the small sawmill that was used for cutting firewood, since a great deal of firewood was needed to keep the flimsily constructed houses warm in winter. The wood was brought in and sold by Chinese immigrants.

What still stands at Bodie covers the full range of the town's activities. There is, for example, the former home of Lester E. Bell, who was in charge of the cyanide plant, then the largest in the United States. The cyanide process, which made it profitable to extract gold from low-grade ore, was perfected in Bodie. Lester Bell's grandson, Bob Bell, was born in Bodie and worked in the mines, and still lives there; his present job is to look after the buildings on behalf of the California Department of Parks and Recreation. After passing shops, houses, the blacksmith's shop, a liquor warehouse and the Masonic Hall, one reaches Chinatown, with its former laundries, food shops, joss house and opium dens. The famous red-light district—Virgin Alley—is now no more than an acre or two of bare ground.

Only the vaults remain of the Bodie Bank, destroyed by fire in 1932. The Assay Office and the Fire-House, too, have gone, but the Post Office and the Schoolhouse are still to be seen and so is the US Land Office, which ended its useful days as a boarding house. The Boone Store and Warehouse, in use for half a century and still standing, was a general store. It sold petrol and paraffin which were brought up from Carson City and Hawthorne in five-gallon cans. When the cans were empty, they were cut up to make covering

Bodie, from the bluff above the Standard Mill, showing the surviving buildings 'preserved in a state of arrested decay'.

for roofs and walls. Two veteran petrol pumps stand by the side of the store, as evidence that the day eventually came when even Bodie was using so much petrol that the can system was inadequate to meet local needs.

To begin with, power for the machinery at the mines came from steam-engines, which burned wood. Coal was not available and eventually wood became so expensive and so difficult to get that an alternative source of power had to be found. A hydro-electric plant was built on Green Creek, twenty kilometres from Bodie, on the assumption (which was as yet unproved) that electricity could be transmitted over wires for a considerable distance. The poles, many of which can still be seen, were put in a straight line, because it was believed at that time that electricity could not turn corners. The system worked and the power station in Bodie has the honour of being the first to transmit over a long-distance line. The engineer responsible was Tom Legget, the superintendent of the Standard Mine, the first in Bodie to operate electric winding gear. The buildings of this remarkable mine, whose success caused the 1878 gold rush in Bodie, have survived, a little battered but more or less intact.

Until the railways reached the remote mining areas of America and Australia, only gold and silver, with their high value and small bulk, were worth thinking about. Once the railways came, however, the situation was transformed. Copper and lead ores could be easily moved away from the mines to the smelters, which were located on good transport routes, and coal could be brought long distances to fuel the furnaces. Sometimes, as at Bodie, the old mining-camp towns died away altogether, sometimes, as at Telluride in Colorado, and Butte in Montana, the early settlements were absorbed into new, prosperous towns, where mining was only part of the total activity. But for half a century, between the beginning of the California gold rush in 1849 and the opening up of the vast deposits in Alaska and the Klondike in the 1890s, large numbers of restless men, many of them immigrants from Europe, saw gold as their one opportunity to escape from poverty and insecurity. For the outside chance of a fortune they risked their lives, stayed filthy and foul-smelling for months on end, lost fingers, toes and noses from frost-bite, spent years existing in the most primitive conditions and, most important of all, established the figure of the gambler, indifferent to personal safety or security and hostile to any Government attempts to control his activities, as an important element in the North American and Australian stereotype.

Few pioneers undertook the miserable journey out to Australia or across America in the hope of making a fortune from lead or copper. It was gold and silver that lured them there, and made the hardships seem worthwhile. The other metals were a bonus, discovered accidentally by the prospectors who happened to be there and exploited by men who had the capital (often acquired by a lucky gold strike, or by selling prospectors supplies and equipment) to install the plant and hire the labour that were needed to extract, process and transport the metallic ores. The bulky metals, such as copper, were not a field in which anyone without considerable financial backing could even begin to operate. Gold, paradoxically, was a poor man's metal. It was also the bait on the hook, without which people would not have come to settle in these harsh regions. Once there, and with communities and the basis of civilisation established, the labour force and the skills existed for other types of mining which proved much more profitable and socially useful in the long run.

Much the same has happened in Europe. The old-established lead and silver-mining centre of Příbram, in Czechoslovakia, is now much more interested in the uranium ores which the miners formerly threw away as a nuisance; and at Falun, in Sweden, which until the eighteenth century produced more copper—at that time a precious metal used for coinage—than anywhere else in the world, the money-makers are now iron pyrites and zinc. Here, as in many important mining towns throughout the world, industrial archaeology consists to a great extent of enormous holes in the ground.

At Falun the ancient-looking buildings are not altogether what they seem. The excellent museum here was formerly the Mine Office, built in the late eighteenth century. Early in the nineteenth century, however, the administration of the company—the Stora Kopparberg, or Great Copper Mine Company—was transferred to the town centre, and the building was allowed to fall into disrepair. In 1922 it was restored to house the museum, but by the 1960s opencast mining made it necessary to move it to a safer site. It had already been damaged by subsidence and could not be preserved in its entirety. The decision was therefore taken to reconstruct it, using as much of the old building as possible. As things turned out, only the roof, bell tower, doors, and some of the furnishings are original.

Around what is called 'the Great Pit'—it is roughly 91 metres deep and 427 metres across—a number of old buildings, in addition to the office, have been preserved as industrial monuments. These include two houses, three buildings containing pit-head gear, two waterwheels and an ore-dressing plant. The site is a complicated one, because it is worked both by open-cast and by underground mining, with a main shaft nearly 610 metres deep.

But the Stora Kopparberg is complicated, too, in the remarkable breadth of the company's interests. It owns, for example, very large areas of forest, which it acquired as a result of Sweden having practically no coal—the great demand for timber for the mine, and for smelting the ore, led to the forests of northern Dalarna being reserved for the needs of the mine. The people of the district paid taxes in the form of deliveries of wood and charcoal to the mine and furnaces. The company bought forest land throughout the eighteenth and nineteenth centuries, often in conjunction with the purchase or establishment of an ironworks. At that time the production of charcoal was very widespread, and both the furnaces and the forges required enormous quantities of it. Today the forests owned by the Stora Kopparberg cover an area of nearly a million acres, and produce pulp, paper and timber for the construction industry, instead of the charcoal for which they were originally intended. They are an important part of the ecology, if not exactly the archaeology of industry. Without them the great copper mine would have been unable to operate in the first place. With them, the Stora Koppar-

View of Falun with the Great Pit in the late eighteenth century. On the right can be seen two sets of wooden rods operating pumps in the mine from waterwheels.

The town square, Falun, from a late eighteenth-century drawing.

berg has been able to diversify and grow into one of the biggest industrial concerns in northern Europe.

The vast hole in the ground at Falun, the old buildings round the edge and the company's huge forest holdings tell most of the story, but a walk round the town of Falun itself helps to put everything into proportion. As one can see from the houses and the public buildings, the miners here have always been privileged people. Unlike the pioneers in the west of Canada and the United States, they have old-established traditions of living comfortably and peaceably, secure under the paternalistic umbrella of a well-managed, benevolent company. Strikes and disputes at Falun have been almost unknown, and the thought of one murder a day would seem to come from another planet.

2

Working with Metals

One of the most important iron-working sites in the world is in England, at Funtley, Hampshire. Funtley is on the River Meon, three kilometres from Fareham and nine from Gosport. There had been a forge here since early in the seventeenth century, and in 1775 it was bought by Henry Cort, who was at that time a Navy agent, with no experience at all of iron-making. It was at Funtley that he developed the puddling process, which allowed wrought iron to be produced much more cheaply and efficiently than was previously possible. His first patent (1783) was for 'a new Mode and Art of Shingling, Welding and Manufacturing Iron and Steel into Barrs, Plates, Rods, and otherwise, of Pure Quality, in large Quantities by a more effectual Application of Fire and Machinery, and with greater yield, than any Method before attained or put in Practice'. This patent was linked to another, also taken out in 1783, for producing rolled shapes of iron by means of grooved reducing rolls. The claim that the new method was more efficient is indisputable. The traditional system produced only a ton of iron in twelve hours; Cort's process produced fifteen tons.

Cort was spurred to develop these processes as a result of a contract he received in 1780 from the Dockyard in Portsmouth for iron hoops for ships' masts, to be made from scrap supplied by the Dockyard. He won the contract by undercutting the other suppliers, who had formed a price-ring to take advantage of the demand following the war with America; but once established as a naval contractor he found difficulties in meeting his obligations. The scrap-iron and the coal for the furnace could be transported fairly easily to Funtley, first up Fareham Creek to Fareham and then by road, but water to

OPPOSITE
Above Reconstruction of installations at the nineteenth-century gold-mine workings at Sovereign Hill, Ballarat.
Below Houses built in Le Creusot for Welsh iron workers and miners in the early nineteenth century.

32

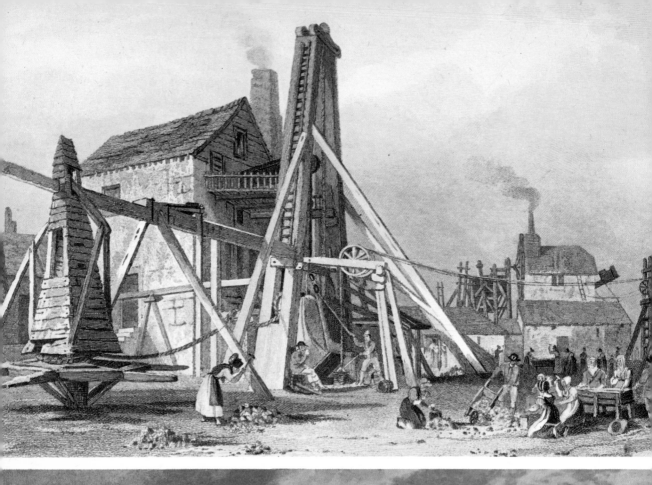

Above Dolcoath copper mine, Camborne, Cornwall, in 1831, when the tin and copper industries were booming.
Below Cort's mill at Funtley. A contemporary watercolour now in possession of the Metal Society.

Puddlers removing a ball of molten iron from the furnace at Thomas Walmsley's foundry at Bolton.

provide the power to drive the rollers and the forge-hammer—the tilt-hammer—was very limited, because of the small size of the River Meon. Recent work by archaeologists has discovered how he made the most of what water was available and what the layout of the buildings was. As a result of this we are now in a much better position to understand the remarkable, even heroic nature of Cort's achievement.

The material the Navy wanted was wrought iron, which is made by heating, hammering and reheating iron several times until it develops the peculiar fibrous structure that gives wrought iron its characteristic strength and resistance to corrosion. In the puddling process, as developed and patented by Cort after his experiments at Funtley, the iron is stirred in a reverberatory furnace, so that the temporary lining of the furnace combines with the iron, helped along by a man called a puddler who uses long-handled paddles to mix the red-hot contents of the furnace thoroughly. When everything is to

his satisfaction, the puddler and his assistant work the iron inside the furnace into what are best described, perhaps, as iron sponges, four or five at a time, each weighing about 50 kilos. These are man-oeuvred through the door of the furnace and dropped on to a small trolley, which takes the iron to the hammer, where it is compacted into an ingot. Then, while still hot, the iron is passed through rollers to produce flat bars. These bars are cut into short sections, which are then packed together, reheated in a separate furnace, and welded together into a single mass by the hammer. Once more through the rollers, and the process is repeated. If wrought-iron scrap is used, instead of pig iron, the reheating and rehammering are not necessary. The iron which is eventually produced is a material of superlative quality, an engineer's iron. In 1975, nearly two hundred years after Cort's invention, the last puddling furnace still working anywhere in the world, in Bolton, Lancashire, closed. The puddler and his assistant there were the last men to make iron this way. When they retired, the process may have died with them. There will be no more wrought iron, unless by a miracle one or two young men can be dis-covered who are willing to learn this very skilled but exceedingly laborious technique. We shall be left only with steel and cast iron, neither of which has the same strength or the same resistance to corrosion.

In Henry Cort's day, however, there was no problem in finding men. Funtley failed to develop as an iron-making centre, however, because the puddling process demands a lot of fuel, both for the fur-naces and for a steam-engine to drive the hammer, and the sources of coal were too far from Hampshire to allow the works to function on an economic basis. Cort himself died in 1800, and it is doubtful if puddling was carried on at the works after that date, but his achieve-ments at Funtley are an interesting example of the stimulus which war can give to technical innovation.

The works closed in the 1850s. The slag which was generously dumped over the site has made subsequent excavation difficult—iron slag is not the easiest of materials to dig through and remove—and a fire which occurred in 1870 destroyed a number of the build-ings. It has, even so, been possible, by combining archaeology with a study of documents, aerial photographs and contemporary water-colour drawings to get a good impression of the works as it was during Cort's lifetime.

The water course system is complicated, and it has clearly been altered at various times during the nineteenth century. It is evident,

Part of Cort's iron furnace, Funtley, excavated in 1964 by a team of sixth-formers from Portsmouth Grammar School.

even so, that what Cort did was to divert the River Meon one kilometre above the mill, and to feed the water into a pond, made by building a dam of soil and lumps of furnace slag. The pond, which was originally over two metres deep, has now entirely silted up. The water was taken from the pond and under what is still called Ironmill Lane by a brick tunnel, which still survives, as does the pit for the undershot waterwheel. There is also evidence of the feeder canal which Cort built to tap two small tributaries of the Meon. These little streams are so small that we can see how desperate Cort was to use every possible means to find more water to drive his hammer and rollers.

The only other survivals of any significance are Henry Cort's house (the inside has recently been completely rebuilt and modernised) and what is now a barn, in one corner of which are the remains of a reverberatory furnace, still with the openings through which the puddlers stirred the iron. This is probably where Cort carried out

35

the experiments which marked an entirely new era in the manufacture of wrought iron and enabled Britain, within a decade, to become the principal iron-producing country in the world.

Le Creusot, the great French centre of pioneer iron-makers, has been more fortunate than Funtley, and there is still much to be seen of the buildings where Louis Bourdon developed what the French claimed was the first steam-hammer in 1848, and where the first French-built locomotive was produced, the *Gironde* (1838). During the Second World War British and American air raids attempted to cripple what was then one of France's principal centres for the manufacture of heavy armaments for the Germans, but most of the bombs missed the ironworks and fell on streets of nineteenth-century houses nearby.

Industrialisation of the district had begun in the eighteenth century, with the establishment of coal-mines at Le Creusot, Blanzy and Montceau and, at Le Creusot, a Royal Iron Foundry and the Royal Factory for making crystal glass, which was transferred from Sèvres in 1784. The opening of the Canal du Centre, which runs nearby, made it possible to export the coal easily and to develop coke-ovens, machine-building and repair workshops and coal-washing plant. The Royal Foundry, however, fell on bad times, and in 1833, when it was owned and run by two Englishmen, Manby and Wilson, it was bought by two brothers, Adolphe (1802–45) and Eugène (1805–73) Schneider, whose name eventually became famous throughout the world for the design and manufacture of guns. The works was greatly extended during the second half of the nineteenth century, housing estates and hospitals were built for the workers, and the Schneider family steadily built up a commercial and financial empire which had connexions and influence all over Europe and which reached the peak of its power in the 1920s and 1930s.

After the Second World War, Le Creusot declined rapidly. The mines were closed, the old products were no longer required and new ones still had to be found, the Schneider family itself faded out of the picture and there was considerable unemployment in the area. During the past ten years, however, successful attempts have been made to pump new life into the old Schneider complex, now no longer under control of the family, and to bring in new industries. At the present time, the town has a very noticeable air of prosperity about it.

What part can archaeology play in helping to reconstruct the

. The Château de la Verrerie, Le Creusot, showing the cones of Marie Antoinette's crystal glassworks in the courtyard, and part of the nineteenth-century Schneider works beyond the trees.

Detail of winding gear
at Pré-Long pit,
Montceau-les-Mines.

history of Le Creusot over this period? It so happens that Le Creusot has what the French call an eco-museum (eco stands for ecological), the Museum of Man and Industry, an original and vigorous institution, which was set up in 1972 to document and study 'the industrial civilisation' of the area and to 'build bridges between those who are still living and those who are long dead'. The Museum is the district itself, an area of something like three hundred square miles, with a population of 150,000. Every factory, house, inhabitant, church, tree, cow and blade of grass is part of the Museum's 'collections'. There is a headquarters, with a small professional staff, elegantly and efficiently housed in the eighteenth-century crystal factory, which subsequently became the Château de la Verrerie, the palace-like home of the Schneider family. The same building contains a permanent exhibition to show how the district has developed over the ages, but this is regarded as no more than a core for the eco-museum proper, which is the district itself. The Le Creusot section of the eco-museum, to consider only one part of it, has a great many buildings and other features which throw light on the way in which local people have lived and worked over the past two hundred years.

There are, for instance, a number of mid-nineteenth-century buildings of the factory itself, including two which are to be preserved as part of the Museum, the former locomotive shop and the foundry. Nearby is a tunnel, which was constructed to allow the members of the administrative staff to go directly from the works to the Schneider mansion without needing to present themselves to the public en route. The town itself was deliberately kept divided into two halves by the Schneiders, as some protection against riots and demonstrations during strikes. The railway and the factory buildings running along the bottom of the valley effectively separated one half of the town from the other, and the single road-bridge spanning the railway provided the only means of communication between the two, almost like a drawbridge across the moat of a medieval castle. Within the next few years, however, this psychological gulf will be overcome by the simple but enormously expensive method of roofing over the valley, including the railway which runs through it, and building a new town centre on a vast concrete platform. For the time being, however, the bridge stands as a token of the pains which the Schneider family took to control the population. Paternalistic in the nineteenth-century manner, they never hesitated to call in troops to suppress strikes. The workers' leaders were tried by judges who

Young women picking stone from coal at Montceau-les-Mines, near Le Creusot, about 1900.

shared the views of the Schneiders themselves, and were sent to prison without the slightest compunction, twenty-five of them in 1870, for example, for sentences of up to three years. The town is generously endowed with statues of various members of the family—there are six altogether—which served as a constant reminder that these father-figures were always at hand, to chastise as well as protect.

On a hillside overlooking the town is a remarkably un-French group of cottages, built early in the nineteenth century to accommodate Welsh miners and ironworkers, who came over with their families to teach industrial skills to the natives. These cottages, built near the pits, still have their original coal-sheds that took the miners' large supply of cheap coal, and the wash-houses at the bottom of each garden that gave the men an opportunity to remove the pit grime before going indoors. The pits here closed many years ago, and the former waste-tips are now covered with trees. The charming little houses, however, are destined to survive, after some interior modernisation, as lodgings for people who want to spend a period carrying out research into some aspect of the history of the area. Many of the other houses built by the Schneiders for their workers were obliterated in the course of a poorly aimed American air raid in 1944, and have been replaced by modern blocks of shops and flats.

39

Statue of Eugène
Schneider, Le Creusot.

By combining a study of the surviving pre-1914 buildings at Le
Creusot and of the material at the Museum headquarters, including
the Château itself, one can obtain a good impression of what life was
like here when a single family ruled the town and when three out of

every five people were employed directly by the company—a situation remembered with a curious mixture of fear and loyalty by old people in Le Creusot, and almost incomprehensible to anyone under the age of forty. But strange and subtle influences of the past persist, even among young people. Until ten years ago, when it was at last thrown open to the public, the splendid park at the Schneiders' palace was strictly reserved for the family. Yet, even now, very few people choose to cross it, even though the road through it represents a considerable saving of time when going from one part of the town to another. The old Keep Out has settled deep into the local psychology.

Company towns and villages based on iron-working were at one time common throughout Europe. One found them especially in Germany, in what is now Czechoslovakia, and in Sweden. A century ago it would hardly have been an exaggeration to describe central Sweden as an area of hundreds of small iron-working settlements separated by patches of forest. It was the hills with their ore deposits and their wood for charcoal-burning which gave birth to these innumerable forges. The settlements sprang up during the eighteenth and nineteenth centuries, particularly along the belt of high-quality ore which stretches from Dannemora, in Uppland, down to Perseberg, in Värmland. The ironworks had to be scattered so that competition for water-power and for supplies of wood could be kept under control. Until the middle of the last century they remained small-scale affairs, owned by a private individual or a family, but with the development of new metallurgical methods conditions changed entirely. It became necessary to merge many of the small concerns and to make large investments in new types of furnaces and machinery. Of the hundreds of ironworks which existed in 1850, no more than fifty still remain in operation. The rest are now only names or ruins, with a decrepit manor house or parts of a blast furnace or a forge as reminders of former activity.

A good example of a works which has survived and prospered is at Surahammar, in Västmanland. There has been a forge here since the late eighteenth century. The modern steelworks, which now belongs to a large engineering group and is no longer the property of a single family, still employs a large proportion of the people who live in the town, and the old paternalistic spirit, very characteristic of Swedish industry, is far from dead even today. It is interesting to notice that the steelworks continues to use the old name, Surahammar Bruk. '*Bruk*' is an almost untranslatable Swedish word. It means, so far as one can find an English equivalent, an industrial settlement or, perhaps better, an industrial manor. One or two of the *bruks* are still to be seen in something like their original form, with the neat rows of workers' houses, the forge, the charcoal store, the shop and the owner's residence. Most of these relics have been swept away at Surahammar, but at one end of the modern plant the company has preserved the early nineteenth-century water-powered forge intact, complete with its tilt-hammers, reducing-rolls and Lancashire reheating furnaces. The meadows and woods running right up to the old forge remind us that, for much of its history, iron-working in Sweden has been a very rural affair, located where there was a reliable river to drive the waterwheels. If one visits Surahammar in the winter, however, the limitations of water-power, at least in a northern climate, become apparent: the river freezes up, the waterwheels have nothing to turn them, and the hammers remain motionless.

The old forge at Surahammar no longer works. It has been preserved in a fossilised condition, with everything weathertight, safe and labelled, but entirely still. A powerful feat of the imagination is needed to recreate the place as it was fifty or a hundred years ago, with the noisy manufacture of railway wagon wheels in full swing and teams of men welding the parts together by hitting the red-hot metal one after the other and chanting a curiously primitive song as they worked.

At Dobřív, in Czechoslovakia, on the other hand, the old forge, very similar in many ways to that in Surahammar, has been maintained in an operating condition, so that visitors can occasionally see the ancient smith—he is over eighty—and his assistant actually at work. To keep one of these forges in an operating condition is no easy thing to do, and it is expensive. Both the hammers and the waterwheels, the hammers especially, contain timber of a size and quality that is nowadays difficult to get, and, whether the country is Sweden, Czechoslovakia or the United States, the necessary skilled labour has almost disappeared. The old craftsmen who have the ability to repair these survivals from yesterday are dying off very fast and there are no young men to take their place. Industrial monuments are, in this respect, no worse off than palaces or churches. How such buildings as London's Westminster Abbey or Vienna's Schönbrunn Palace are to be maintained and repaired in the future is a problem which so far remains no closer to a solution.

But to see a waterwheel actually working and operating the

Wrought-iron sign
now in the National
Technical Museum,
Prague.

machinery in a mill or a workshop that it was designed to power is an experience not to be missed. It is only then that one can really understand and respect the skill of the eighteenth- and nineteenth-century millwrights and engineers, who worked very largely by eye and with tools that seem primitive by modern standards. But the simplicity and reliability of the machinery they built is an important part of its effectiveness and charm. These great tilt-hammers had heads weighing up to 150 kilos, but all day long, ten times a minute, the cams on the shaft connected to the waterwheel lifted them up and let them drop on a piece of red-hot iron held underneath by the smith's tongs. When one sees them doing this, as is still possible at Dobřív, they have the appearance of great birds pecking at grain, but they pecked to some purpose for centuries, producing the wrought iron that was in constant demand by engineers and toolmakers everywhere.

There was a forge at Dobřív in the fifteenth century and it continued in operation until 1956, making and mending agricultural tools for the local community. There are three waterwheels, two to drive the hammers and one for the bellows which provides blast for the forge. A small room at the end of the building was used for

43

The colonnade at Marienbad.

storing beer for the smiths—a reminder of the heat and weariness which went with the job.

The Central Bohemian region, between Prague and Plzeň, has been famous for its iron-working skills since the Middle Ages. During the eighteenth century major changes took place as a result of the increasing timber shortage. Casting required less fuel than wrought iron production, because the metal does not have to be reheated, so that from about 1750 onwards Bohemian ironworks turned increasingly to cast-iron products and reached a level of technique that was unequalled anywhere in Europe. A number of museums in Czechoslovakia have examples of the miraculously delicate work that was achieved early in the nineteenth century—bracelets, necklaces, brooches, dishes, memorials, stoves, window-frames and many other articles. The Komárov foundry was especially famous for this type of work, which is much sought after by collectors. Nowadays it concentrates, more prosaically, on water-pipes and bath-tubs.

There are many survivals, too, of the splendid large-scale work produced by the iron-founders of Bohemia and Moravia during the nineteenth century. One of the most remarkable examples is the great colonnade at Mariánske Lázně (Marienbad), built by the Blansko Ironworks in 1889 and still in excellent condition, but there are also superbly designed railings, bridges and fountains to testify to the extraordinary craftsmanship of the Czech school of iron-founders. When one thinks of the small size of the blast furnaces which turned out these objects in great quantity between 1750 and 1850 (much bigger foundries came into existence only during the second half of the nineteenth century) the achievement becomes even more impressive. One of these early blast furnaces, at Adamov, in Moravia, has survived in a reasonably complete state. The furnace, which dates from 1752, is built of stone, square-sectioned and tapering towards the top. It is scheduled as a national monument.

The European techniques for working iron were transferred to America during the seventeenth and eighteenth centuries, and in recent years great efforts have been made to preserve and reconstruct the ironworks which survive from this period. The Saugus Ironworks, in Massachusetts, set up by Joseph Jenks in 1646 to manufacture scythes, has been recreated on its original site after excavations had revealed the plan of the buildings. Jenks defined his aim as 'the speedy dispatch of much work with few men's labour in a little time', and this has remained the aim of American industry ever since. The Saugus Works included a blast furnace, foundry, forge, rolling-mill and slitting-mill, all of which have been rebuilt and re-equipped, so that visitors can now get a good idea of the techniques and scale of iron-working in the early Colonial period. The iron-master's house, built in 1648, still survives, together with the boarding house which Jenks put up three years later to house a group of immigrant workers from Scotland. Saugus operated for only twenty-two years, but it was of great importance in the industrial development of the colonies; it acted as a kind of technical college, where a number of men who subsequently set up as iron-masters on their own account were trained.

America has preserved several of its early iron-working villages. Hopewell, in Pennsylvania, made iron from 1770 until 1883. Visitors to what is now classified as a National Historic Site can see the furnace, the iron-master's house, and a number of other buildings belonging to the industrial complex. Speedwell Village, in New Jersey, made and worked iron from the 1770s. Between 1814 and 1873 the Vail family had a foundry and machine shop here, their products including the engine and machinery for the famous steam-ship, *Savannah*. Much of the plant used during the Vails' ownership of the works still remains. In Allaire State Park, New Jersey, one can see the restored Howell Ironworks (1830) and Allaire Village, a self-contained iron-working community, an American *bruk*, which produced its own food and clothing, made most of its own tools, furniture and vehicles, looked after its own fuel supplies, and settled easily and inoffensively into the rural landscape. Canada, too, has a *bruk*, the village of the St Maurice Ironworks, at Trois Rivières, Quebec, which dates from the eighteenth century, and has been well restored.

All these ironworks used local ore and local charcoal. Without the forests, which the American colonists burned in such a reckless and prodigal fashion, they would never have existed. But, as a visit to Hopewell or Speedwell makes clear, each works was very small. Until well into the nineteenth century it was rare to find one employing more than fifty men. Those great iron-eaters, railways and automobiles, had not yet arrived, and even war devoured metal on what seems, to a twentieth-century mind, a nursery scale. One of the best illustrations of this is the former Bellona Arsenal, at Midlothian, Virginia. The Arsenal, founded in 1815, consisted only of one foundry and four workshops. In 1942 the remaining buildings were restored and converted into a single house—an indication of the domestic size of the original works.

Once iron had become really big business, with coal as the fuel and the railways and the army as the most important customers, the works were for the most part no longer located in rural areas. This means that the archaeology has been continuously obliterated, as new techniques were developed and more up-to-date works built. In the country there was less incentive to pull down the old works and re-use the site. This is as true of America as it is of Britain or Germany. There is another difficulty if one tries to use archaeology to recreate the past of iron- and steel-making, a difficulty which is much greater now than it would have been thirty years ago—the old centres have been cleaned up in a way that would at one time have seemed impossible. Concern about pollution has removed the pall of filthy smoke from Pittsburgh, Sheffield and Essen, so that the industrial or social historian has to make a real effort to imagine what conditions were like as recently as the 1940s. Soot-coated buildings used to be taken for granted as part of the industrial scene, but this is no longer true, and the cleaning-up process has removed an important link between the twentieth century and the nineteenth. In the United States, environmental considerations have already closed a coke furnace, the Sloss Furnace No. 1, at Birmingham, Alabama. The furnace, built in 1882, was shut down in 1970 because the serious pollution could not be overcome. It is now classified and cared for as an industrial monument, one of the largest objects in the world to receive this accolade. No other country in the world has so

The furnace, 1830, at Howell Ironworks, Allaire State Park, New Jersey.

far decided to preserve a technological relic of this size, but in this case only time can show how far 'preservation' is possible.

One ever-present difficulty in saving industrial relics from destruction is that, so often, their historic interest is only realised a long time after they have been scrapped. What has happened in the Cornish tin industry shows this very well. For most of the nineteenth century, the industry prospered. The tin ore was mined, crushed in strange machines known as Cornish stamps which pounded the ore with batteries of heavy iron bars, raised and allowed to fall by means of a roller equipped with cams; and then washed and shaken to sort out the tin from the arsenic and the waste. After new and more cheaply worked sources of tin were discovered in the Far East and in

47

OPPOSITE
Exterior of the forge
at Dobřív, Czechoslo-
vakia.

South America, Cornish tin production virtually disappeared. Then, about ten years ago, the world price for tin rose to such a level that it became economic once more to develop and modernise the mines in Cornwall. Anyone exploring the area around Redruth found himself confronted with huge areas of ruined tinworks, mostly with their chimneys still standing, and dumps of mining waste, the whole scene looking as if a major air raid had taken place a few years previously. And there, against a background of the ruins, is a modern mine which is doing very well. The whole district, until recent road developments obliterated much of the archaeology, was a splendid laboratory for studying the industrial history of Cornwall.

A vital part of the archaeology would certainly have disappeared for ever but for the initiative and public spirit of a man newly retired from running a road haulage business in Birmingham, Philip Welch. Mr Welch bought a former tin-streaming valley, more than 3 kilometres long, and set about restoring the old plant and bringing it back into production as the Tolgus Tin Company. Eight years' determined work and a great deal of cannibalism—rebuilding one machine from the remains of several others—have produced what most people would have felt safe in saying had gone for ever, a traditional Cornish tinworks. The raw material (the heaps of waste from the old mines) costs almost nothing. All Mr Welch has to do is to bring lorryloads of it to his works, mix it with water and run the resulting slurry round a fascinating system of revolving tables and shaking tables until the useless material has been removed and the tin ore has been concentrated to a point at which it can be smelted.

The attraction of this method, the traditional one, of working the tin ore is that the small man can use material which the large concern cannot be bothered with. Visitors—several hundred a day during the holiday months—enjoy their guided tours round the works and are happy to buy what the smelter produces, tiny ingots of pure tin. The combination of entrance fees, sales of tin and profits from refreshments and publications finances the whole operation, an enterprising piece of living industrial archaeology. It is safe to say that without Mr Welch's initiative there would now be no survivor of the celebrated Cornish stamps or round-frames. Fifty years ago there were hundreds of each, working or abandoned.

It is interesting to notice in this connexion that only one other example of a traditional tin processing plant is known to exist in Europe, at Altenberg, in East Germany. This building and its equipment is believed to date back to the sixteenth century. It had

The Danish Mill
Board's workshop
centre near Odense.

become semi-derelict and between 1954 and 1958 a large restoration
programme was undertaken to preserve it in working condition. Like
the Tolgus Tin Company, Altenberg has the advantage of being in a
popular tourist area and reckons to have as many as 80,000 visitors
each year. The plant is now driven by electric motors, not by its
original waterwheel, and is divided into three parts: the long row of
stamps to crush the ore to a fine powder, the washing-tables and the
furnaces to smelt it. The stamps, constructed largely of wood, are of
a more primitive type than are found in Cornwall. Under the processing building, part of one of the mine galleries has been made
accessible to visitors.

The installations at Tolgus and Altenberg illustrate a tendency
which is becoming more marked each year within the field of
industrial archaeology—to make machinery work wherever possible.
This has not been universally welcomed; there are those who feel
that old machines are much too precious to be worn out to please the
public, and that replicas should always be used for such a purpose.
To this the enthusiasts for operating machinery reply that if parts
wear out, they can always be replaced and that there is no essential
difference between fitting new parts into an old steam-engine or
waterwheel and restoring the stonework in a cathedral. What is certain, however, is that restoring and maintaining industrial monuments, whether the machines are working or not, is a very expensive
business and that the more people can be persuaded to pay to visit
them, the more likely they are to survive.

In the case of steam-engines, which are always immensely
popular, there is one factor which makes it extremely unlikely that
they will be driven to a premature death—the present price of coal.
At two British sites, Crofton, in Wiltshire, and Ryhope, in County
Durham, the practice is to put the magnificent engines there under
steam on one or two selected weekends in the year, and this seems
to be a very sensible way of solving the problem. But, even when
these fine beam-engines are silent, the visitor is unlikely to feel
cheated.

Crofton Pumping Station, near Great Bedwyn, in Wiltshire, is on
the Kennet and Avon Canal, at one time one of Britain's most
important cross-country waterways. The pumping station was built
during the first decade of the nineteenth century to supply a 55-
kilometre stretch of the canal between Bedwyn and Seend with its
water, which had to be raised twelve metres from a natural reservoir,
Wilton Water, to the summit level of the canal at Lock 55. It had the

Parallel motion linkage of 1812. Boulton and Watt beam-engine at Crofton Pumping Station.

secondary function of providing water for Lord Ailesbury's mansion, a few miles away. Two engines were required. The first, which began pumping in 1809, was built by Boulton and Watt at their Soho, Birmingham, foundry in 1807 for the West India Dock, but was diverted to the canal company the following year. The second, and more powerful—42 against 37·6 h.p.—engine is also by Boulton and Watt, and was installed in 1812. In 1844 improvements were made to both engines by the famous Cornish engine builders, Harvey's of Hayle, and later in 1844 a Sims engine was ordered to replace the 1807 engine. This gave a good deal of trouble, and was eventually rebuilt, with a new cylinder.

The boilers were replaced in 1905, and the pumps themselves were in regular use until 1952; operating simultaneously, the pumps could lift twenty-nine million litres in twenty-four hours. No. 1 engine, the Sims, was in steam as late as 1958. Both engines were completed to a high degree of finish and throughout their working life they were well maintained. Much of the maintenance and cleaning was carried out by apprentices from the Railway Workshops at Swindon.

The Kennet and Avon Canal Trust acquired the pumping station from British Waterways in 1968 and restoration work was immediately put in hand. Financed by contributions from the Government, local authorities, engineering institutions and other bodies, it was carried out by a remarkable variety of volunteer experts in engineering, boiler-making and pump maintenance, and by working parties from Aylesbury Prison. The aim was admirably stated by one of Britain's greatest writers on engineering history, the late L. T. C. Rolt. 'Until you have seen one of these huge engines at work,' he wrote, 'it is impossible to appreciate their majesty fully. As the great beam rocks to and fro in its trunnions high overhead, the down plunge of the piston rod and the polished geometry of the Watt linkage, in the poetry of their mechanical motion, seem the most perfect expression of controlled power. Take steam away, and their breath of life is gone, bright metal tarnishes and the engine house goes cold and dead.'

Two equally fine and equally well cared for engines can be seen at Ryhope Pumping Station in County Durham. This very beautiful pumping station supplied water to Sunderland and South Shields for a hundred years, using beam pumping engines manufactured in

The beams of the 1812 (*right*) and 1840 (*left*) engines at Crofton.

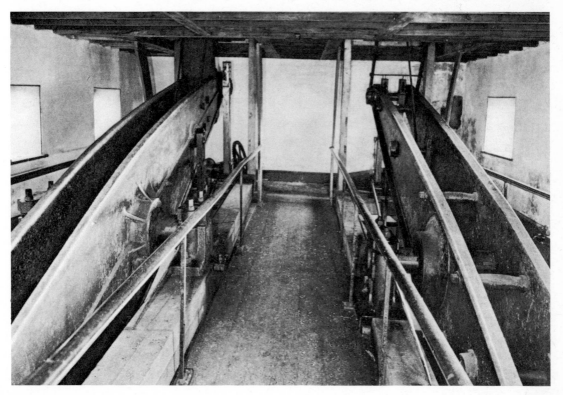

OPPOSITE
The pumping engines
at Ryhope.

1868 by R. and C. Hawthorn of Newcastle upon Tyne. The engines worked completely reliably for the whole of their period of service, delivering a steady 120,000 litres an hour, and they have been preserved as part of a Museum of Water Pumping, with one engine left capable of working and the other powered by electricity for everyday display purposes. Nothing has been destroyed or removed. One can still see, in addition to the engine-house and boiler-house and the superb chimney—perhaps the most graceful in Britain—the houses for the engineers, the entrance gates—more reminiscent of a ducal palace than a pumping station—and the smaller of two reservoirs. The main reservoir, with its pleasantly scalloped edges, was roofed over some years ago, to keep out leaves and other wind-brought debris.

There are several ways of considering Ryhope. The steam-engine enthusiast may be interested to know that the engines are double-acting rotative compounds, with Watt parallel motion and centrifugal governors, and that the high-pressure cylinders are of 698·50 mm bore and 1·625 metres stroke, and the low-pressure cylinders 1·143 metres bore and 2·438 metres stroke. The information that the operating pressure is 2·5 kgs per sq cm and the vacuum in the condensers 660·40 metres may also be invaluable to him. More ordinary visitors—and Ryhope receives a good many thousands of them each year—are likely to be impressed by the fact that a hundred years ago a water authority was designing and commissioning buildings of such outstanding architectural quality, and that the engine manufacturers gave so much attention to detail. The Victorians, as Ryhope Pumping Station makes clear, made no distinction whatever between art and utility. They did each job as perfectly and as patiently as they knew how. One of the most important functions of industrial archaeology is to give us the opportunity to understand our ancestors' values a little better. We preserve things, in and out of museums, in order to inform ourselves about what people made one hundred or two hundred years ago, and in order to give ourselves an opportunity to ask and to answer the really significant question, 'Why did they do it like this?'

3

Factories and Mills

Three things can happen to an old factory, once its owners decide to take a careful look at it in order to assess if it is earning its keep. It can be modernised, possibly structurally, and certainly with new machinery. It can be made over to some completely different use. Or it can be closed completely, and either demolished or allowed to tumble down. In this chapter we shall be looking at examples of each of these possibilities, bearing in mind that certain kinds of structure are more likely to be fortunate than others. An old gasworks, for instance, is an old gasworks, and it is extremely difficult to think of any other use for it. A bridge is a bridge. And a gunpowder works is a gunpowder works, built in a particular way to meet a particular need; once it ceases to make what it was designed to make, the only answer would seem to be to pull it down. If anything of it should eventually happen to be preserved, we can count that something of an archaeological miracle.

Such a miracle occurred at Faversham, in Kent. Faversham has a good claim to be the birthplace of the British gunpowder industry. The first factory here started operating at some time before 1558. Before that time England imported all her gunpowder from the Continent. The choice of Faversham was not accidental. To begin with, a Tudor gunpowder factory had to be in the South of England, where the royal arsenals and dockyards were. If it had been in the North or the Midlands, transport costs would have been prohibitive. Then there was the question of raw materials. Gunpowder has three ingredients; saltpetre, sulphur and charcoal. Saltpetre came mostly from Italy and India, and sulphur from Italy, so it was essential, given the conditions of road transport in the sixteenth century, that

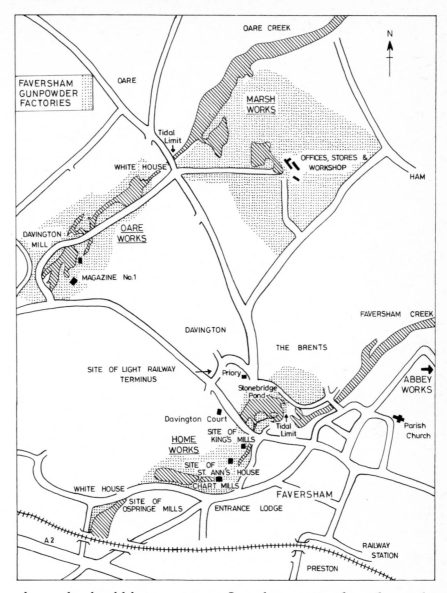

The remains of the Faversham Gunpowder Factory today.

the works should be near a port. It took two tons of wood to make enough charcoal for one ton of gunpowder, so it was very desirable that the factory should be close to suitable woodlands. Faversham met all the requirements.

The original works, later known as the Home Works, was established on what is now known as St Ann's Estate. Soon afterwards another works, the Oare Works, was set up by the side of the Home Works, and both continued to prosper, under several changes of ownership, until 1760, when the Government decided to have a gunpowder factory of its own instead of relying entirely on private suppliers. The Home Works at Faversham was taken over as the Royal Gunpowder Factory in that year and a large programme of extensions and improvements was begun.

Among the improvements were measures for limiting the effects of blast should an explosion occur. The early manufacturing techniques had been primitive, using first a pestle and mortar to mix the powder and then stamp-mills, in which the mixture was pounded by mechanical hammers driven by horse- or water-power. This hammering was particularly likely to cause explosions. There was a very bad one in 1724, described by Daniel Defoe: 'The blast was not only frightful,' he wrote, 'but it shatter'd the whole town, broke the windows, blew down chimneys, and gable-ends not a few; also several people were killed at the powder-house itself, tho' not any, as I remember, in the town.' The use of stamp-mills was finally forbidden by Act of Parliament in 1772, but for many years before that the larger mills, such as Faversham, had been using what were known as edge-runner mills, in which heavy stones rolled round over the powder, which was placed in a circular stone trough.

In an attempt to contain the force of an explosion, eighteenth-century gunpowder works built thick walls in strategic positions and planted belts of trees which would eventually have the same effect. Today, these trees—or those which have survived—are in their prime, and at Faversham the magnificent cedar, oak, ash and beech trees, which were originally thought of as a safety precaution, are now, with the factories long closed, an important part of the amenities of the district. But the authorities at the Royal Gunpowder Factory did not rely on trees, walls and edge-runners alone to protect the works and the locality from disaster. A set of rules, issued in 1785, were the model for all future rule-books in the industry. The aim was to do everything possible to prevent a spark from occurring, and to this end all the machinery and even the hinges on the doors were to be kept well oiled, workmen were forbidden to wear their own shoes on the premises, barrels had to be brushed to make sure no grit was on them, the ground over which the powder-carts ran had to be covered with brick rubble, to prevent possible danger from flints, and the metalwork on wheelbarrows had to be of copper, not iron.

After the Napoleonic Wars the works went back to private ownership, and from then until 1934, when production finally came to an end, there were several interesting innovations—gun-cotton in 1846 (Faversham had the first gun-cotton factory in the world); pellets in

Volunteers excavating
Chart Gunpowder
Mills, Home Works,
Faversham.

1876; nitro-glycerine in 1892; cordite in 1892. But despite strict precautions, including the placing of buildings at some distance from one another and the building of protective mounds of earth between them, there were also some terrible accidents, including a particularly bad one in 1916 when over one hundred people lost their lives in a TNT explosion.

Most of the factory buildings have now disappeared, but as a result of planned demolition, not accidental explosions. Gravel working has obliterated some of the sites, although a number of the eighteenth-century houses survive. The most important remains are at Chart Mills, in the heart of the old Royal Factory complex. Here, in the middle of a modern housing estate, are four mills where the mixture was ground, the only examples left in Britain. When reconstruction began in the 1960s, three of the mills had lost most of their equipment, but the fourth was almost complete, looking very much as it did in the eighteenth century, with its waterwheel and its massive machinery. The very active Faversham Society has restored

the whole group, the aim being 'to recreate the mills authentically in their setting, giving the impression not of a lifeless museum-piece, but of active machinery which has just been stopped for an inspection'. It is not permanently stopped however: on special occasions the waterwheel runs and the mill grinds, not gunpowder, but a harmless concoction based on sawdust.

What has happened at Faversham to preserve this historic site is not, it should be noted, as a result of any interest shown by the last owners, Imperial Chemical Industries, although this is a very rich and influential concern. The fact that we can now see this group of mills operating is entirely due to the initiative of a private society. The situation at the equally remarkable gunpowder mills on the Brandywine River—the Eleutherian Mills—near Wilmington in Delaware, has been quite different.

These mills were established by Eleuthère Irénée du Pont, who arrived in America in 1799. By 1811 his mills on the Brandywine had become the largest industrial enterprise in America, with a profit in that year of $45,000, an unusual amount for the time. Du Ponts today are not the biggest company in America, but they are firmly in the top league and—an important factor in the survival of the Eleutherian Mills—the family has continued to live in the area, with mansions and estates at Winterthur. The preservation of the Brandywine Mills has been very much a du Pont affair. The little stone-built, water-driven mills (there are twenty of them) were spread out for safety along the river bank, and they have been excellently restored or 'stabilised', but the project has not been confined to them. The Brandywine Village Historic District, with its well-preserved houses (mainly of the late eighteenth century) and its shops and flour mills, puts the gunpowder business in a meaningful local context.

E. I. du Pont's impressive stone and stucco house, built in 1803 and now open to the public, is furnished in a style which reflects the changing tastes and interests of five generations of the mill-owner's family. By the side of the house is a small building which, until 1890, served as the du Pont Company office. It has now been restored to its mid-nineteenth-century office appearance, with clerks' desks, high stools, a wood stove and whale-oil lamps. The President's office is furnished with original pieces, including the Presidential desk, powder containers and a carpet bag used by a salesman to carry samples. Near the house is a large barn, which formerly housed company and family vehicles and was the centre of

A pair of restored powder mills on the Brandywine River.

The Du Pont black powder mills on the Brandywine River.

the estate farm. It has now been restored and a museum of wagons, carriages and farm implements is established in it.

The company's first professional chemist was Lammot du Pont, the grandson of the founder. His experiments were conducted a mile or so away in a small workshop which has now been moved to a site nearer the house and furnished with the equipment in use in the mid-nineteenth century. E. I. du Pont was a keen gardener and botanist. After the family moved from the Eleutherian Mills in 1890, the garden became overgrown and eventually all evidence of it disappeared. It has now been restored, following excavations which revealed the original paths, the well, and the foundations of the hot-houses, cold frames and gazebo.

The du Ponts did very well for themselves. Gunpowder was a highly profitable commodity, a fact evidenced not only by the personal fortunes of entrepreneurs such as Eleuthère du Pont, but by the great houses they built for themselves, which are just as significant a part of the archaeology of gunpowder as the mills are. Apart from the du Pont residences at Winterthur, there is a remarkable small palace at Haverford, Pennsylvania, where another of America's leading gunpowder manufacturers based himself. His mansion, appropriately called Nitre Hall, still survives, together with the powder magazine.

Nitre Hall and the Brandywine have enough material still remaining above ground to make both the physical and the mental reconstruction of the industrial past a relatively easy matter. At other sites a greater effort is required. The Caughley Porcelain Works, near Broseley in Shropshire, is an example of a place where the archaeologist had to work hard to bring together information from every possible source, at a time when the site was about to be totally destroyed by open-cast clay-working.

The factory was established in 1754, initially to produce earthenware. Soon afterwards it began to make porcelain of the finest quality. In 1780 Thomas Turner, the proprietor, visited porcelain factories in France and brought back several skilled workmen with him. The very successful Broseley Blue Dragon design was in production by 1782 and in 1790 Turner perfected a bright violet-blue underglaze decoration, which also proved popular. In 1799 Turner retired, and sold his business to one of his former apprentices, John Rose, who had a factory at Coalport, the home of the celebrated Coalport porcelain. The notice in *Eddowes Salopian Journal*, announcing the sale of his stock by auction, said:

> 'The stock consists of a great number of beautiful tea and coffee equipages of various much approved patterns, in full and short sets, richly executed in enamel and burnished gold, together with a great variety of elegant blue and white tea and coffee sets, table and dessert services, muffin plates, butter tubs, etc. Mugs, jugs, egg cups and drainers, butter cups, custard cups of different sorts and sizes, pickle shells, eye baths, asparagus servers, toy tables, tea sets and candlesticks, etc., in pearl white with a great variety of other articles both useful and ornamental.'

Rose eventually found the Caughley factory uneconomic to run and concentrated his activities at Coalport, on the opposite bank of the Severn. In 1814 Caughley was closed and the materials from it were ferried across the river to enlarge the Coalport factory.

In 1964, when open-cast clay-working was about to obliterate the site, Dr A. W. J. Houghton surveyed it with the excavators and bulldozers hard on his heels. What he found showed that Caughley had

Blue dragon pattern on Caughley porcelain.

produced a much wider range of pottery than the written evidence suggested. Dr Houghton's investigation was a model of archaeological detection. He noticed to begin with that the two tracks leading from the factory site to the river were scattered with fragments of Caughley ware, both glazed and unglazed. Since the men preparing for the excavation of clay on the factory site had found only three small pits containing broken pottery, Dr Houghton very reasonably concluded that the normal practice had been to dump the rubbish in the river.

Where the factory had been, he came across a great deal of material which had been used in making and firing the pottery. There were broken saggars (the dishes on which pottery was stacked for transfer to the kiln), and large quantities of separator rings, which were placed between one object and another during firing. Large flints were scattered about, for grinding and mixing with the clay, which would have been kaolin, brought by sea and river from Cornwall (the local clay is suitable for making bricks and drainpipes, but not fine porcelain). There were also lumps of gypsum lying around, to be used for making moulds.

Among the sherds, Dr Houghton found earthenware of various colours, glazed and unglazed, and quantities of decorated porcelain, some with polychrome decoration. A few pieces of French and Chinese porcelain also came to light, suggesting that fine quality examples were imported so that the English workmen could copy the designs. Some of the fragments of Caughley ware were decorated with gold lines and stars, which shows that gilding was not, as traditionally supposed, carried out only in London. The great variety of types and patterns found on the site shows that Caughley found a market, or perhaps created one, for goods which came between the luxury porcelain made in the eighteenth century by a few small concerns and the mass-produced articles which met the taste of the affluent middle-class of the early Victorian period. Its blue-and-white tea and dinner services symbolise this. As the dumps of broken pieces on the site showed, Caughley blue-and-white was of a consistently high quality—ladies with social aspirations had no reason to be ashamed of possessing it—and yet produced in large enough quantities to keep the price reasonably low.

A similar piece of detective work was undertaken in 1962 by Geoffrey Lewis at the Catcliffe Glassworks, near Sheffield. The twelve-metre brick cone here has been a local landmark since it was built in 1740. Mr Lewis, with a team from the Sheffield City Museum, excavated the flue and other parts of the cone in 1962, when it was believed that demolition was imminent. Fortunately, however, representations to what was then the Ministry of Works (now the Department of the Environment) were successful and the cone, the only one to survive in anything like a complete state, is now officially scheduled as an industrial monument.

These conical glasshouses, which were in fashion in England and the Weser region of Germany from about 1730 until 1850, were complete working units, not just kilns, in which all the working processes took place, from melting the glass to annealing the final product. The tall building with its small roof acted as a chimney, and the openings round the base provided an adequate draught. The furnace, which contained the pots of glass, was in the centre of the floor area and the other work connected with glass-making went on around it. A similar cone, which lost its top half many years ago, still exists in Bristol. Until the mid-1960s it was used by a firm of fertiliser manufacturers for mixing and storing compound fertilisers. The site was then bought by a hotel company, which restored the old cone and now uses it as the main restaurant for its new hotel, the *Dragonara*. This restaurant is now the only remaining building of the once important Bristol glass industry.

At Catcliffe, the archaeologists had a good deal more to work on —and were able to add a bit more. The history of the glasshouse was already fairly well known, from its establishment in 1740 until its closure some time between 1884 and 1887. Bottles dated later than this were, however, discovered during the excavations and an old man who had once worked at Catcliffe and who had read in the local paper about Mr Lewis's investigations confirmed that the works had, in fact, been subsequently reopened for a very brief period. He said that another firm started making bottles there in 1900 and went bankrupt within a year. Reference to a local directory confirmed this. The firm is listed for 1901 only.

None of the glass found during the excavations dates from earlier than the middle of the nineteenth century. The broken glass from the furnace flue was mainly coloured bottles. Careful examination showed that none of it had been made at Catcliffe and that all of it was later than 1887. The style was characteristic of the first decade of the present century and the names on the bottles included those of three Sheffield firms, a wine and spirit merchant, a chemist and druggist, and a brewer. All these firms were flourishing in 1900 and it became clear that this glass had been bought for remelting as what glass-makers call cullet—scrap glass—during the brief re-opening of Catcliffe at the turn of the century. The research at Catcliffe provides a good illustration of the value of combining three sorts of evidence: material from excavations; written history; and reminiscences of old workers.

An interesting piece of intercontinental detective work took place during 1966–67. It concerned an early nineteenth-century woollen mill at Bathurst, Eastern Province, South Africa. An architect in practice at Grahamstown wrote to me, saying that he had recently surveyed the mill as a preliminary step towards restoration by a South African foundation which exists to preserve and rehabilitate all types of industrial monuments. The architect wanted to discover more about the builder of the mill, Samuel Bradshaw, who was believed to have emigrated to South Africa from Gloucestershire in England; and he was also anxious to obtain details of the type of machinery with which Bradshaw would have been familiar and which he would have installed in his mill at Bathurst. The intention of the Trust was to buy or make equipment which would give as accurate an impression as possible of the mill as it was in its working days. This meant that, by an odd trick of history, the most complete representation of a nineteenth-century Gloucestershire mill would eventually be found in South Africa.

All that was known then was that in 1820, although some of the Hottentot people in the area had sheep which had been obtained for them by missionaries, there was no way of processing the wool mechanically. The situation changed when Samuel Bradshaw, thirty-six years of age and a weaver, landed in South Africa on April 30th 1820, as the leader of a party of emigrants from Gloucestershire. He built the mill, with the intention of producing blankets.

Bradshaw is a rare name in Gloucestershire, but a series of lucky clues led to the village of Cam, where the parish registers yielded

The restored Bradshaw Wool Mill, Bathurst, South Africa.

the fact that Samuel Bradshaw had been baptised there in 1784. As a result of the decline of the local cloth trade many people emigrated from Cam between 1820 and 1830, mostly to America. Bradshaw and his group were exceptional in choosing South Africa.

In 1820 the woollen trade in the West of England was half-way between the old home-industry and the modern factory. The yarn-making was carried out in the factory; the weaving in the home; and the finishing again in the factory. The mill at Bathurst would have followed this pattern. It would have been what was known as a scribbling and fulling mill, preparing the yarn and fulling the cloth. The settlers would in all probability have had to make the machinery themselves, although it is just possible that, since the party is known to have included a number of skilled weavers, they brought some items with them. By 1966 everything had gone from the old mill, and to make it operational once more, machines of the old type had to be copied from museum pieces in England.

Preserving a mill six and a half metres long and five metres wide, as at Bathurst, is one thing, but preserving over one and a half kms of mills, on both sides of a river, is quite another. This was the problem that faced the great American textile manufacturing towns of Manchester, in New Hampshire, and Lowell, Massachusetts, and both towns have found it insoluble. By the end of the 1930s, the mill-owners had begun to transfer their operations to the Southern states, where union difficulties were less serious and where manufacturing could take place in new, single-storey buildings that were better suited to modern needs. The New England mills were abandoned one by one, either to fall into dereliction or to find themselves divided up into a number of smaller factories. By the 1960s both the planning authorities and the local population had become tired of having so much unwanted, neglected property on their doorsteps, and a wide-ranging programme of demolition became inevitable. During the past five years, acres of mill buildings and workers' lodging houses have been flattened, and many of the most important and characteristic monuments of nineteenth-century industrial America have vanished from the scene.

Forewarned of what was about to happen, the Smithsonian Institution, the Merrimack Valley Textile Museum and the National Park Service co-operated in a mammoth and very professional survey of a number of the more historically interesting mills. This is certainly the most ambitious industrial archaeology project ever to have been organised, and it was carried through successfully during two summers, 1967 and 1968. In the time available it was not possible to survey every textile mill in New England—Lowell, for instance, had to be omitted entirely—but what was achieved has illustrated the value of co-operation and good management if adequate records are to be made before the evidence is swept away. The photographs, architectural drawings and written research material have all been deposited in the Library of Congress in Washington, so that they can be readily consulted by the general public, and they have also been edited into a book, published by the Historic American Buildings Survey. This is the kind of survey and recording work which is, as yet, very rare in industrial archaeology.

Each section in the survey says exactly where the mill was located, who the owners and occupiers were, what it was used for and what its historical significance is. A typical entry here would be, for the Harris Mill, Harrisville, New Hampshire:

'The earliest surviving woollen mill in the village, it was built by Milan Harris in 1832–1833. It is a rare example of pre-"slow-burning" mill construction, with its joist floor-framing and top "trap door" clerestory windows.'

There is a brief history of the mill, a note of any articles that have been written about it, a detailed description of its construction— this is backed up by photographs and drawings—and an account of its condition when the survey was carried out. Any surviving machines or fittings are mentioned, and, in the case of the Harris Mill, the team has noted, 'There are no sanitary facilities in the building,' which is the kind of useful information normally over-

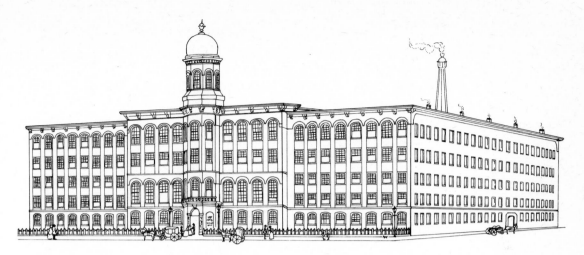

The Chickering piano factory in Boston from a mid-nineteenth-century print.

looked by industrial archaeologists, who are apt to mention only what exists and to forget what does not exist.

If projects like the New England Mill Survey had been carried out extensively in all the major industrialised countries during the past fifty years, we should now be much better equipped to recreate an accurate picture of how our ancestors earned a living. One sad aspect of this particular survey should be mentioned—there was no time and no money to collect the memories of men and women who had worked in the mills. The result, inevitably, is archaeology without people, a weakness which the organisers fully realise.

Few old industrial premises have been as fortunate as the former Chickering piano factory, at 791 Tremont, Boston, Massachusetts. Five storeys high and covering two and a half acres, it was built in 1853 for Jonas Chickering, who had scored a great success with his exhibit at the Great Exhibition in London two years earlier, and at the time it was opened it was the second largest building in America (the first was the US Capitol in Washington). It had 23,250 square metres of enclosed space, with a vast, 2,090 square metres inner courtyard—the size of a football field. Americans are very fond of statistics and like to mention that Chickering's splendidly constructed piano palace required, among other items, three million bricks; 503,000 metres of timber; 11,000 panes of glass; 18 kilometres of iron piping; 300 barrels of nails and 24,180 square metres of flooring. At one time the company was turning out more than 400 pianos a day, with its own clipper ship to bring rosewood and mahogany from South America.

Chickering's piano manufacturing came to an end in the 1930s and the great factory was then rented out in bits to a number of different firms—an organ and piano repairing workshop, laundries, a harpsichord manufacturer, several furniture makers, a picture-frame maker, the *New England Free Press*, and many others. For forty years practically no maintenance was carried out, but the building remained structurally sound. Early in 1971 a young Boston architect, Simeon Bruner, happened to be giving a face-lift to one of the furniture showrooms in the old factory and it occurred to him that 791 Tremont would be ideal for an artists' housing project, which he and his friend, Bob Gelardin, a planner and relocation expert, had been thinking about for some time. Their idea was to design large open living units which painters, sculptors and musicians could arrange to meet their own particular working requirements. Only bathroom and kitchen fixtures would be provided, and movable cupboards to serve as room dividers.

Bruner and Gelardin bought the building and persuaded the Massachusetts Housing Finance Agency to grant them a three million dollar loan to convert it. No attempt was made to disguise the fact that it was a factory. Brick walls were left unplastered and wooden beams exposed, and fitments were arranged so as to prevent the iron columns supporting the ceilings from coming in the middle of the kitchen or bathroom. Studios for people like musicians and sculptors, whose occupations involve a good deal of noise, were acoustically treated. Wide doors and lifts and outsize drains were provided, to get bulky materials in and up, and stone chippings and other working debris away. Dark-rooms were installed, the basement was converted into an exhibition area, every apartment was connected with a master television aerial, and a restaurant, meeting rooms and parking-spaces were added to the amenities. The only thing missing, one might suggest, is something which will surely come in time—a small museum devoted to Chickering and his pianos, to act as a bridge between the past and the present.

Without a boldly conceived project of this kind, the Chickering factory, one of Boston's most notable landmarks for more than a century, would certainly have had to be demolished. As matters worked out, however, the building was saved and several hundred artists and craftsmen and their families have been very satisfactorily housed. The same solution to a growing problem would undoubtedly find an equally warm welcome in Paris, London, or any other large urban area. It would also allow a number of historic industrial buildings, no longer needed for their original purpose but in good structural condition, to be saved.

Studio conversions in the Chickering piano factory.

The Chickering factory may have been an interesting building and its disappearance would certainly have removed one of Boston's most familiar sights; but piano-manufacturing is not, as yet, a branch of industry which has attracted any marked amount of nostalgia or enthusiasm among preservationists. Without doubt the most popular lines so far, the ones with most fans, have been railways, windmills and watermills, in that order. Every country in Europe has a considerable number of surviving watermills in varying states of repair, and, for the most part, rather fewer windmills. Windmills are more exposed and go to pieces quicker once they are no longer used and maintenance has stopped. Watermills have often been adapted to other uses. They can sometimes be converted into pleasant houses and they can be found carrying out a wide range of

69

functions as farm-buildings. It is rare nowadays to come across one with its old machinery intact, and even rarer to be able to see a mill still grinding corn. During the past fifty years milling has become a highly centralised affair, mainly concentrated at the major ports, and most of the inland mills, of whatever age or size, have been driven out of business.

No country has tried harder or more systematically than Denmark to preserve some of its typical mills in working order. In 1953 the National Museum set up a Mill Preservation Board, with the aim of preserving a selected number of mills on their original sites. Several had already been moved to open-air museums, but that is not at all the same thing. From its early days the head of the Board has been Anders Jespersen, an engineer who is probably the greatest living authority on the traditional type of mill; a complete enthusiast whose life is totally dedicated to mills. He is a great believer in keeping the mill functioning wherever possible, with a State subsidy if necessary, and as proof of this he himself has bought and restored a beautiful seventeenth-century watermill and miller's house on the island of Fyn, and made it his home. Several other public-spirited Danes have done the same thing, spending a great deal of their own money on restoring the buildings and the wooden machinery of an old mill while there are still craftsmen around who can carry out the work. A local engineer has, for example, saved Børkop Mill in Jutland. Built in 1830, this large mill, with two waterwheels, was close to collapse in 1959 when Mr Christoffersen bought it and brought it back into working order, with a subsidy from the Mill Board. This mill was chosen for the special watermill stamp, which was issued by the Danish Post Office in May 1962, as a token of the practical interest which the Government was showing in restoring these important relics of the country's industrial past.

Nybjerg Mill is also in Jutland. It was built in 1850 and a century later it was bought as a semi-ruin by a businessman, who spent £7,000 of his own money on restoring it and bringing it back into use. The work here included digging out the mill-pond again, after it had been allowed to run dry and to spend twenty-five years as a meadow.

For the past five years, the Mill Board has had its own workshop centre, suitably located at an old windmill near Odense. Here a small group of skilled craftsmen has been got together, with one or two apprentices, stocks of timber have been built up—some of the largest pieces are gifts from the State forests—and specialised machinery

Stamp showing Børkop Mill, Jutland.

Brede Works, Denmark, near the home of the Danish Mill Board.

installed to allow the work to be accomplished with the greatest efficiency and at the lowest cost. This workshop centre is a model for what will eventually have to be achieved elsewhere, if old industrial plant is to be repaired and maintained in an age in which the necessary craftsmen are almost ceasing to exist. By concentrating all one's resources at a single point, as the Danes have done for their mills, a school of craftsmen can be built up and apprentices given a proper training. Work can then be undertaken on contract for old buildings or machines which are in need of expert attention. Such schemes are being discussed in a number of countries—by the Smithsonian Institution in Washington, for example, and by the Ironbridge Gorge Museum Trust in Britain—but Denmark has got there first.

The Danish Mill Board practises what it preaches. Its own headquarters, in the Brede Works, not far from Copenhagen, is in one of the most interesting old factory buildings in Denmark. There was a watermill on the site in the fourteenth century, probably used by the skinners to grind oak-bark for tanning their hides. In 1628 a gunpowder mill was set up there, for crushing and mixing the charcoal, sulphur and saltpetre. This lasted for forty years and in 1668 a copper-works replaced the gunpowder works and operated until 1810, producing pots and pans and other brass and copper utensils, together with scythes. At that point the works underwent great changes, being transformed into Modeweg's textile factory. The first steam-engine was introduced in 1840 and shortly afterwards the first

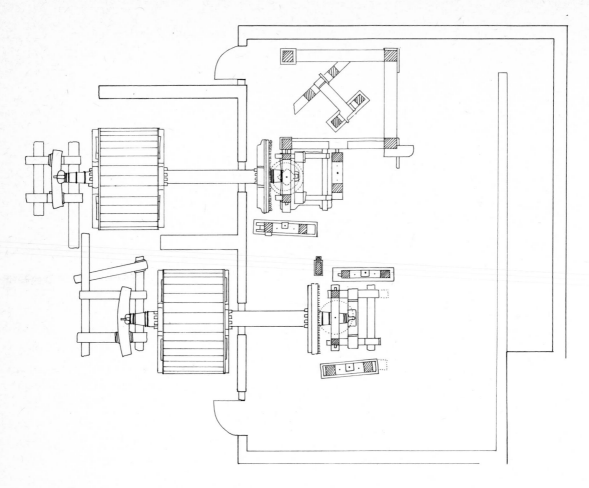

Plan of the water-
wheels and gearing at
Børkop Mill.

water-turbines and power looms. Modeweg's went out of business in
1956 and the Government bought the buildings, partly as an administrative headquarters for the Mill Board and partly as a store, and
eventually a museum, for old machinery. It was a wise choice. In
addition to being beautiful in themselves, the buildings are most
attractively situated in wooded surroundings, with the great mill-
pond stretching out in front. There are few industrial sites anywhere which have a longer and more varied history, and few which
convey more strongly the feeling of what industry was like in its
rural, water-powered days. The peaceful Mølleaa—Mill River—on
which the Brede Works stands was the most important industrial
area of Denmark during the seventeenth, eighteenth and nineteenth centuries, with nine mills producing cereals, paper, cotton,
cloth, iron, starch, copper and brass, gunpowder and agricultural
implements. Brede has to be visited and thought about within the
context of the whole area, and as evidence that in a country with no

coal and plenty of water it was still profitable, even towards the latter part of the nineteenth century, to develop new industry on a basis of water-power and water-power alone. On the Mølleaa, turbines were cheaper to run than steam-engines.

Denmark, like Switzerland and Canada, is a fortunate country in that it has suffered hardly any damage from war for a very long time. The destruction of old buildings has been the result of a deliberate modernisation policy, not of bombs and invading armies. Industrial plants in Denmark were not destroyed in air raids, as they were in Poland, Germany, Britain and the Balkans. The industrial archaeology of war-ravaged countries is liable to be unbalanced; water-mills, stone quarries and workshops in the countryside have a better chance of survival than factories in urban target areas.

Romania illustrates this situation very well. This is a country with rich oil and gas reserves. The use of oil drawn from natural springs has been recorded there since the fifteenth century, although no attempt was made to bore for it until the 1820s, when the first well was mechanically drilled, using wooden rods and the Canadian percussion system. The pioneering Romanian petroleum distillery was commissioned in 1857 at Rîfov, near Ploieşti, to supply paraffin to the city of Bucharest, the first place in the world to have this type of street lighting. With the growth of automobile transport, production increased rapidly during the 1920s and '30s, but during the 1939–45 war enormous damage was done by air raids and the Romanian oil industry virtually ceased to exist. The Petroleum Museum at Ploieşti, which deals with the history of the extraction and use of petroleum, is very much a matter of models and diagrams. Any archaeology of the early days of the industry which survived until 1939 (and there was not much—wooden derricks and wooden huts are very impermanent affairs) was thoroughly dealt with by American bombers.

But, and this is the important point, Romania had no other industry of any size before 1945. Since the nation's resources were socialised in 1945, industrial development has been very rapid. By 1968, the volume of industrial production had risen to ten times the 1938 figure, with sixty-five per cent of the machinery needed by its industries being produced at home. Exactly the same is true of Yugoslavia, Bulgaria and Hungary. In all these countries, the Industrial Revolution came more than 150 years later than it did in Britain, and for this reason the cotton mills, engineering works, canals and iron foundries which were common enough here and which are part of the stock-in-trade of our industrial historians and archaeologists simply did not exist in countries which only emerged from a backward peasant economy when the political system changed. Early industrial buildings in countries like Romania date from the late 1940s and early 1950s, not from 1800. Apart from little rural windmills and watermills, this is where their industrial archaeology begins.

A survey carried out in Bulgaria in 1878 showed how completely dependent the country then was on agriculture and handicrafts, with only twenty enterprises that could reasonably be called factories. Ten of them produced food or beverages, four textiles, five leather or furs, and one was concerned with metal-working. Even as late as 1914, twenty-six per cent of all Bulgarian goods were made in people's homes, fifty per cent in what were called 'artisan workshops', and only twenty-four per cent in factories. In 1945 the number of craftsmen working on their own, or with one or two assistants, was higher than in 1920.

In these circumstances, one has to have an elastic definition of 'industrial monument'. Bor, in Yugoslavia, offers a good example. Yugoslavia now produces more copper than any other country. The copper mining and smelting works at Bor have been important since the 1920s, although the history of mining in the area goes back to prehistoric times. Photographs taken in 1905 show only a small settlement of wooden buildings, but there was considerable development during the next ten years, mostly with French capital. The installations were almost totally destroyed during the war and the most interesting piece of history, if not archaeology, to be seen there now is the plaque commemorating the handing over of the plant to the control of the workers in 1964. Similar plaques are to be found at many other factories and mines in Yugoslavia, marking a turning-point in the industrial history of the country.

4

Transport

Transport, whether by water, roads, railways or aeroplanes, undoubtedly attracts the interest of more people than any other branch of industrial history or archaeology. There are canal societies, railway societies, aeroplane societies and steamship societies in every country, East and West of the Iron Curtain and on both sides of the Atlantic. Yet when one looks carefully at their activities, it is evident that these are fairly selective. Railway enthusiasts, for instance, are intensely interested in locomotives, rolling stock and signalling, but hardly at all in station refreshment rooms, waiting-rooms, platform construction or ticket offices. Aviation fans are passionate about pilots and aeroplanes, but airports and in-flight meals tend to leave them cold. Canal people can never hear and see enough about locks, barges and viaducts, but appear to have little interest to spare for the health, education and wages of the men and their families who operated the boats. This is sad, but understandable. A steam-engine is more eye-catching and exciting than a waiting-room. But to concentrate only on the dramatic survivals of an industry is to miss half the story, and certainly to get one's proportions seriously wrong.

As an example of a half-story, let us take Swindon in England. Swindon has always been a holy place for British railway fans—the locomotive building and repairing centre of Brunel's Great Western Railway, the home territory of such great engineers as Churchyard and Stanier, the technical base of a railway system which, in Victorian times, had the highest operating standards in the world. With the railway works now only a shadow of its former great self and with the railway no longer the main employer in the town, Swindon has to be content, from a railway point of view, to rest on

its laurels. Because of this wind-down and of the large amount of demolition which has taken place, the past twenty years have been a period of crucial importance in recording railway history. There has been no need to bother overmuch about locomotives, operating methods and so on. These details, the fashionable items of railwayana, have been well cared for by the Museum of British Transport, and by the Great Western Railway Museum, in Swindon. What is much more vulnerable, and much more easily overlooked, is the railway's bricks and mortar—the old station and workshops, the railway village—and the memories of the men on whose skills the Great Western once depended.

The line from London to Bristol was opened as far as Swindon in December 1840. Two months later the Directors announced that they had decided to

'. . . provide an Engine Establishment at Swindon, commensurate with the wants of the Company, where a change of Engines may be advantageously made, and the trains stopped for the purpose of the Passengers taking Refreshment, as in the case at Wolverton on the London and Birmingham Railway. The Establishment there would also comprehend the large repairing shops for the Locomotive Department, and this circumstance rendered it necessary to arrange for the building of Cottages, etc., for the residence of the many persons employed in the service of the Company.'

The 'cottages', which still survive, became an important and attractive housing project, superior in many ways to the vast Corporation estates which have characterised the expansion of Swindon since the war. They were designed by Sir Matthew Digby Wyatt, the architect of Paddington Station, and built by J. and C. Rigby of London, who were already building many of the Great Western stations. The railway was short of money, and the contractors agreed to recover their costs from the tenants' rents. A now somewhat faded water-colour in the Great Western Museum shows an aerial perspective of the estate under construction. From this one can see how a whole street was built at a time. After the bricklayers and stone-masons had got one terrace of houses up to eaves-level, they moved on to the foundations of the next street and the carpenters got busy with the roof-timbering of the first one. The major railway contractors obviously knew their business.

The houses were faced with local stone and were of different sizes, some with two bedrooms and some with three. The corner

The backs of houses in the railway village, Swindon, before modernisation.

77

houses at each end of a street were larger, for foremen, but on two corners a public house was substituted for a foreman's house. Since three hundred houses were planned, the ration was one public house to one hundred and fifty houses. A house, however, is not just a building. It is a place where people live, and in this particular instance we know a great deal about who and how many the people were from the lists of tenants preserved in the British Rail archives. These show that in the 1840s and '50s it was by no means uncommon for a four-roomed house to have ten people living in it, including lodgers, and that some had a dozen. With the outbreaks of cholera and typhoid which occurred from time to time in New Swindon, mainly as a result of the poor water supply, living conditions in these pleasant-looking little terraces must have been trying on occasions, a fact which no doubt explains the rapid turnover of tenants, who moved to private housing further away and preferably up the hill, as the green fields between Old Swindon on the hill and New Swindon down in the valley became covered with the speculative builders' red brick.

But, by the working-class standards of the 1840s, the railway cottages were exceptionally good houses. The outside coal-houses, privies and wash-houses are not the sort of amenities we expect in the 1970s, and the absence of garages does not match up to the expectations of railway workers today; a century ago, however, they formed part of the Great Western Railway's wish to look after its employees in the best way they could. The company built a large Mechanics' Institute with a good library, a covered market, a school, a hospital and, of course, a church. There was a system of free medical attention, paid holidays and sickness benefit, advantages which made the railwayman a highly privileged person. But he paid a price for his privileges, as old employees at the Works well remember. There was an iron discipline in and around the workshop, with fines for bad work, bad timekeeping, eating or drinking at work, or disobedience of any kind. Once inside the boundary wall, the workman had to stay inside; and he was strictly forbidden to enter railway property except through the main gate. Large sections of this great, prison-like brick wall are still there, as awful reminders of a time when the railway management ruled by fear and looked for no other way of preserving discipline. This is certainly the opinion of men who earned their living at Swindon Works before the First World War. They took the bullying and the pressurising for granted and did what they could to defend themselves against it, recognising

Building retaining
walls for the railway
cutting near Park
Street, Camden Town,
1836. The scene in
this drawing by J. C.
Bourne was described
by Charles Dickens in
a famous passage in
Dombey and Son.

that a malicious and unscrupulous foreman had no difficulty in interpreting the rules in a way that suited him. With plenty of unemployment for men on the other side of the wall and hardly any work for women at any time, it was safer to touch one's cap to the foreman than to argue with him. But it was their Works, not the Chief Mechanical Engineer's Works. Without their skills, the drawings and the Board Meetings would have got nowhere at all, a thought which is common enough today but was highly unfashionable fifty or a hundred years ago.

Since 1966, British Rail has sold off the railway village in two stages, first, to the Swindon Borough Council, and then to its successor, the Borough of Thamesdown. The houses were by this time in a poor condition and many of them were empty. The new owners decided to renovate and modernise them, which they have now done with great success. The foremen's houses have each been divided into two flats, but all the rest have been kept as individual dwellings. Elderly people predominate among the tenants and the proportion of car-owners is low, which makes the lack of garages or garage-spaces of no importance. The biggest change has been to sweep away the old outbuildings and yard walls at the back and to give direct access to the back entrances of the houses through a paved precinct. This undoubtedly removes a great deal of history, but it helps to provide houses which modern people are happy to live in. It seems a perfectly acceptable compromise, since the alternative would have been to demolish the houses altogether. Half the

79

archaeology, inside and outside, has been sacrificed in order to preserve the other half.

The old Swindon station, so much cursed and so much laughed at, has gone completely in the past three years, except for a fragment of one of the platform blocks, which is now hidden away below the cut-price facelift which is all British Rail found itself able to afford for Swindon when it was eventually forced to bring the station up to date.

Swindon station never aroused great enthusiasm among architectural historians but, for two reasons, it was very interesting from a social point of view. From the beginning, most of the passengers who used the station would be railway workers and their families, travelling at reduced rates. There was therefore no reason to provide anything more than minimal facilities and a very basic station building. Swindon, so to speak, got what it deserved. At Bristol and Bath, on the other hand, the situation was quite different. These were important cities, with a great many well-to-do people travelling to and from them. They consequently had to be given distinguished railway stations.

But there were complications at Swindon, because on occasions the station had to cater for very elevated persons indeed. From the early days the buildings included a small hotel, which had its bed-rooms on the first floor of the up-side platform block and its dining-room and drawing-room on the down-side. The two parts of the hotel were connected by a footbridge. It so happened that the Prince of Wales, later Edward VII, had a number of friends in the Swindon–Marlborough area and, being an extremely sociable man, he enjoyed meeting them whenever possible. The Director of the Great Western therefore improved the hotel reception rooms at the company's expense, to make them more suitable for royal entertaining. The new amenities included, somewhat surprisingly, a masonic temple. The Prince and his party came down from London or Windsor in a special train, which was kept parked on a siding, the Prince of Wales' racing and land-owning friends drove in to Swindon, where, after a convivial evening together, those who were able to go home did and the others were laid out to cool in the bedrooms once used by the refreshment-room staff. It was an economical, convenient and patriotic arrangement, well known to at least some of the railwaymen in Swindon, but well concealed from everyone else. The present writer was supplied with full details of the scheme by an old lady, one of the last survivors of the famous Gibson girls, who

The façade of the Gare du Nord, Paris.

had often attended these Swindon evenings and who subsequently inherited a racing stable on the Berkshire Downs: which shows that the industrial archaeologist has to cast his net very wide in pursuit of important information.

The point of these revelations about top-level banqueting in Swindon station is not to provide additional material for a future biography of Edward VII, but to show how new facts can make an otherwise dull building interesting and significant. The building itself was demolished in 1972. There were, inevitably, complaints from railway enthusiasts that a precious part of our railway heritage was being destroyed, but none from bodies concerned with the preservation of historic buildings or from the British Tourist Authority. If the facts had been widely known, which they were not, Swindon station, with the old hotel suitably converted into a royal annexe of the Great Western Museum, could have become a considerable tourist attraction.

The kind of railway stations which do attract campaigns for preservation, sometimes successful, sometimes not, are mostly the

grand ones—the Gare du Nord in Paris, Manchester Central and
Penn Central, New York. Some of these railway palaces are truly
remarkable. Buildings such as the Central Station at Antwerp,
the Gare d'Orsay in Paris and Union Station, Washington DC,
employed the best architects and craftsmen available and there was
no stinting on materials. These were the prestige places of their day,
the nineteenth-century airports and corporation headquarters, and
no expense was spared to make them impressive. To have stood inside one and looked up and around is to understand the status which
railways once occupied and occupy, alas, no longer. This status continued until the outbreak of the 1939–45 war. Once the war ended,
the car and the aeroplane began to take over. Nobody will ever build
a regardless-of-expense railway station again. But to remind us how
recently the old tradition ended, there is the Bénédictines Station at
Limoges in France, a noble palace of white stone, with a clock tower
and central dome. Completed in 1929, it is one of the finest examples
of railway architecture to be found anywhere in Europe.

On the whole, the European stations have a much better chance of
survival. The once-splendid railway system of the United States is
now in a sadly run-down condition, with few passenger trains still
operating and the track poorly maintained. A good deal of imagination is needed to recapture the feeling of what these railways were
like fifty or a hundred years ago, when they had a monopoly of long-
distance transport and when they were a source of national pride.
There are clues to past grandeurs, however—palatial but now hardly
used stations, as at Pittsburgh, and the gigantic steam-engines which
are preserved in museums up and down the country. More typical
than Pittsburgh, however, are the crumbling shells, many of them
wooden, of the thousands of small country stations, which have been
out of use for many years now, but which remain as symbols of the
enormous importance of the railways in breaking down the remote-
ness of rural areas and in providing America with its first national
transport system.

This is true of all countries, unfortunately: the notable stations are
kept, mainly because they serve large cities and are therefore still
in use, and the small stations become casualties. The twenty-first
century is not likely to have a very good chance of seeing what a
country station looked like, except perhaps in Norway, where the
open-air Railway Museum, at Hamar, has a number of rural station
buildings, including a station-master's house, furnished and fitted
out as they were in their working days. Without such survivals,

A country station at Helen's Bay, Co. Down, Ireland, 1882, in Scottish baronial style, strongly influenced by the ideas of the Marquis of Dufferin and Ava.

people are unlikely to appreciate the atmosphere created by the heavy benches and tables, coal fires, dark green and chocolate paint and brown linoleum in the waiting-rooms and by the dim gas lighting and Victorian sanitary-ware lavatories which gave railway travel its special image.

Some railway museums have attempted to solve two problems at once by setting themselves up in old stations or engine sheds. In America, the National Railroad Museum at Oneonta, New York, occupies the old Ulster and Delaware Station (1902), and among the other numerous museums in old stations are those at Bucksport, Maine; Union, Illinois; Ashland, Kansas, which specialises in the Santa Fé Railroad; and Howell, Michigan. In Baltimore, the Baltimore and Ohio Transportation Museum is in an old passenger coach roundhouse. Europe has shown similar good sense in one or two places. The Netherlands Railway Museum, for instance, is well housed in an 1874 station at Utrecht and in Czechoslovakia a small historical museum has been assembled in the terminus at České Budějovice of the old horse-railway which was built between 1825

83

and 1832 and used to run to Linz. One of the most original ways of preserving an historic railway station can be seen at Brunswick, in the German Federal Republic. The original Brunswick station, built in 1843–44, is the oldest to survive in Germany. It is no longer in use as a railway station, and in 1960, after being damaged by wartime air raids, it was bought by the Brunswick Bank, which restored it and converted it successfully into the headquarters of the Bank. Something very similar has been achieved in Ottawa, where the fine Central Station was left marooned in the middle of the city, after the railway terminus had been transferred to a new and simpler building further out. With the tracks and the train shed gone, the station entrance hall, offices and refreshment rooms have begun a new life as Ottawa's main conference centre.

But railway monuments are not only a matter of stations and workshops. The nineteenth-century engineers deserve to be remembered just as much, if not more, for the bridges, tunnels and cuttings without which the railway would have had no existence. These works, enormous for any period, were carried out, we should never forget, very largely by human and animal muscle-power. The contractors used whatever machinery they could get, but most of the prodigious amount of excavation needed was done, at least during the first twenty years of railway building, by pick-and-shovel labour. A great many men worked together on each stretch of the line. They were well disciplined, well paid and they worked exceedingly hard. A gang of these railway navvies was an impressive sight. A time-keeper employed by one of Britain's leading contractors, Thomas Brassey, remembered the scene:

> 'I think as fine a spectacle as any man could witness, is to see a cutting in full operation, with about twenty wagons being filled, every man at his post, and every man with his shirt open, working in the heat of the day, the gangers looking about, and everything going like clockwork. Another thing that called forth remarks was the complete silence that prevailed among the men.'

Accidents were frequent, especially in the tunnels, and, with the contractors trying hard to keep to their schedule, both working and living conditions could be very bad.

During the boring of the Woodhead Tunnel, for the line from Sheffield to Manchester, between 1839 and 1845, thirty-two men were killed, and well over two hundred seriously injured. These figures, as the social reformer, Edwin Chadwick, pointed out were,

Building the Box Moor
Embankment on the
Great Western, June
1837. Drawing by
J. C. Bourne.

'. . . nearly equal to the proportionate casualties of a campaign or a
severe battle. The losses in this one work may be stated as more
than three per cent of killed, and fourteen per cent wounded. The
deaths (according to the official returns) in the four battles,
Talavera, Salamanca, Vittoria and Waterloo, were only 2·11 per
cent of privates; and in the last four months of the Peninsular War
the mortality of privates in battle was 4·2 per cent, of disease
11·9 per cent.'

And, appropriately enough, there is a tablet at the end of the tunnel,
in memory of the men who died building it.

In fairness it should be pointed out that the casualty rate at Woodhead was exceptionally high, even by railway-building standards,
and the management was certainly not of the best. The company
paid no compensation to the families of men killed, which contractors of better repute, such as Brassey, would have thought dis-
graceful. But, as we have said, the wages were good and the navvies,
like the gold prospectors of the Klondike, thought the money made
the risk worth while. These were the men who made possible engineering feats which were superior to the building of the Pyramids.
Nothing before the railways had ever been on such a gigantic scale,
and the motorways of the 1950s and '60s do not begin to compete,
as feats of engineering, with Robert Stephenson's London and

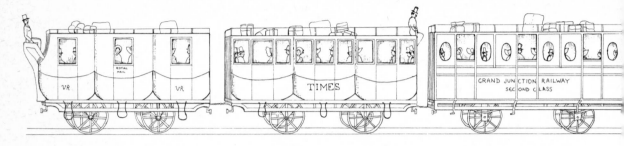

Passengers and mixed
freight on the Grand
Junction Railway in
the 1830s.

Birmingham railway. Modern travellers take the tunnels, embankments and cuttings for granted. For them the railways, unlike motorways and hill forts, just happened. Brunel and Stephenson said, 'Let there be a railway,' and there was a railway. For some curious reason, the achievements of the railway builders in North America, both the engineers and the men who did the work, have been much more successfully glamourised and publicised. There have been many films of the driving-the-last-spike-with-buffaloes-and-Indians-looking-on type, and half a century of films have pushed the message home. Yet, in their different way, the achievements of the English railway navvies, both at home, on the Continent and as far away as the Crimea, were quite as remarkable and heroic as those of the labourers in the United States and Canada, and, it might be suggested, quite as worthy of the attention of film-makers.

There is certainly a great deal more interest to be obtained from a railway journey if one thinks of the constructional problems involved along the route and of the amount of sheer backbreaking toil that was needed to cut through that hill or to throw up an embankment across this marsh or valley. The matter of materials also deserves more than a passing thought. In Western Europe, there was, in general, no serious difficulty in finding reasonably accessible

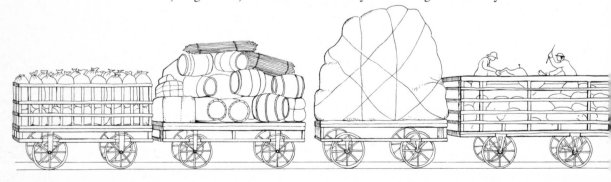

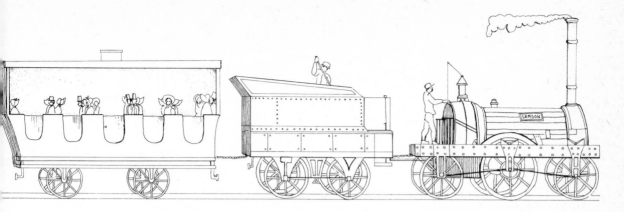

stone quarries and beds of clay for making bricks, but in America the situation was quite different. There, and in Russia, railways had to be built very much on the cheap. Finance was hard to find and savings had to be made in every possible way. This meant steeper gradients, to avoid the expense of deep cuttings, timber viaducts and bridges, low platforms, and, outside the main cities, primitive stations. There was no money for the workmanship, finish and refinements that were accepted as normal in Britain. The recipe in big countries—Australia, Canada, Russia, the United States—had to be 'The minimum expenditure for the quickest return'. Later, perhaps, it might be possible to improve the system in a number of ways, but, to begin with, the cheaper the better.

When railway building started in Britain there was a heavy tax on bricks (5s 10d a thousand), which was not abolished until 1850. One result of the brick tax was that the building of the canals and early railways and of many mills and factories was made a good deal more expensive than it need have been. There was also a powerful incentive to use stone wherever possible. The railways were very important customers of the brickmakers. In 1821, before railway building began, the number of bricks charged with duty in Britain amounted to 913,231,000. By 1831 the total had risen to

OPPOSITE
The Barentin Viaduct.

1,153,048,581—the tax authorities believed in accuracy—and by 1840 to 1,725,628,333. It is not difficult to see why such immense numbers of bricks were needed. A turnpike road bridge over a railway required 300,000 bricks, and a railway tunnel 8,000 for every yard of its length, or about 14,000,000 a mile. It is important to remember in this connexion that until the middle of the nineteenth century all these millions of bricks were hand-made, by a moulder who threw clay into wooden moulds, one brick at a time. The British process known as wire-cutting, by which a slab of clay was cut into bricks by dragging a taut wire through it, was not invented until 1841. The first extruding machine is reputed to have been made and used near Bridgwater, Somerset, in 1875. It was extremely simple: extrusion was carried out by means of a shaft which pushed the mass of clay between knives placed at right angles to one another.

Two of the most distinguished pieces of railway brickwork in the world are the Barentin Viaduct, nineteen kilometres from Rouen, and the Göltzschtal Viaduct, between Reichenbach and Plauen, in the German Democratic Republic. They are roughly contemporary, the first being completed in 1846 and the second in 1851. Both are still in regular use.

The Barentin Viaduct was built, as part of his contract for the Rouen–Le Havre line, by Thomas Brassey, who carried out a great deal of railway construction on the Continent as well as in his native Britain. It crosses a deep valley, on a fairly sharp curve, and its twenty-seven arches are about thirty metres high. Six days after it had been completed, it collapsed after several days of torrential rain. The reason was never established, but two suggestions made at the time both seem possible; the first, poor mortar and the second, filling the track bed with ballast before the mortar in the viaduct was properly dry. In a very anti-British atmosphere produced by the accident, Brassey was accused of being interested only in taking as much money as possible out of France and of doing work of poor quality in order to increase his profits. To meet these charges he announced that he would rebuild the viaduct entirely at his own expense—a not inconsiderable matter of £30,000. Finding another eight million bricks and a different source of lime in a hurry was far from easy, but it was somehow managed with the same English bricklayers as before, and having completed the whole railway three months ahead of schedule, Brassey received a bonus of £10,000 from the grateful railway company and, what was even more acceptable, a refund of his £30,000.

The Göltzschtal
Viaduct.

Brassey was a railway enthusiast, a man who believed passionately
in railways as a civilising influence. In his opinion the more railways
there were, the higher the standard of living in each country would
inevitably become. But in addition to this crusading faith, he wanted
to be recognised as the greatest railway contractor of all time, the
man with most work in hand and the man who always finished on
time. He demanded, and got, a very high standard of workmanship
and the results are clear. The graceful Barentin Viaduct is still standing and still carrying traffic a hundred and thirty years after it was
built. The only maintenance it has needed has been the re-pointing
of the brickwork.

The Göltzschtal Viaduct has stood up equally well. With its three
rows of arches, it is remarkably like the great Roman aqueducts, such
as the Pont du Gard in Provence. The reason for the similarity is not
sentimental or romantic. This design, perfected by the Romans two
thousand years ago, combines maximum strength and low wind
resistance with minimum quantity of materials and, until steel
became readily available in the latter part of the nineteenth century,
there was no reason to look for anything better.

For viaducts of this length the Americans, who were short of
bricks, stone, cement and skilled workmen, would certainly have
used timber during the 1840s and '50s, as Brunel did for similar

90

constructions on the line between Plymouth and Penzance. But for shorter bridges, pre-fabricated wrought-iron spans were increasingly used in America from 1850 onwards, often to replace earlier timber or stone bridges which had become dangerous or which had been washed away. One of the best known designers of these iron trusses was the Baltimore engineer, Wendel Bollman. Few examples of his work still survive, but one, at Savage, Maryland, is almost certainly the oldest remaining non-stone railway bridge in the United States. It stands near a large cotton mill that began operating in 1815 and was erected to carry the Savage branch off the Baltimore and Ohio's Washington to Baltimore main line, which was opened in 1835.

Robert M. Vogel, of the Smithsonian Institution in Washington, has done a great deal of research into the history and technical development of American railway bridges, and he has managed to solve a number of puzzling problems connected with the Bollman bridge at Savage—in particular, its age. The owners of the cotton mill, it appeared, took the first opportunity of having a spur connexion laid to the branch line, as a means of transporting both raw materials and finished goods. To begin with, they used a wooden trestle bridge to carry the track over the Little Patuxent River, but in 1850, before the Civil War, they succeeded in obtaining one of Bollman's experimental iron trusses and this did good service here until the 1880s, when the mill was extended and a re-alignment of the track and bridge became necessary, and another Bollman bridge, the surviving one, was brought second-hand from somewhere else and installed over the Little Patuxent River.

By that time there were about a hundred Bollman spans on the Baltimore and Ohio and its subsidiaries. In the years following the Civil War there was an urgent need for bridges, both as replacements for those worn, destroyed or damaged during the war and for new work, and the Bollman design, which could be fabricated, transported and erected easily and quickly, was ideal for the purpose. Some of them were made at the Baltimore and Ohio's works at Mount Clare, and some by Bollman's own bridge company at Canton, Baltimore. The Savage bridge, so far as Mr Vogel has been able to discover, was produced at Mount Clare, Baltimore, in 1869 and was first used at some point between Baltimore and Ohio, the exact site still being unknown. In 1887, it was moved to Savage.

The detective work leading to these conclusions has been ingenious. Photographs exist of other Bollman bridges built during the 1869–70 period—the bridges themselves disappeared long ago—and

The Bollman truss bridge at Savage, Maryland.

a careful study of them shows that on the decorative portal at each end they had six cast-iron strips screwed to the main casting. These strips carried, in raised letters, the following inscriptions:

Top left W. BOLLMAN, PATENTEE
Bottom left BALTIMORE, MARYLAND
Top centre BUILT BY B. & O. R. R. CO.
Bottom centre Year of fabrication
Top right PATENTED 1852
Bottom right RENEWED 1866 (i.e. the patent, not the bridge)

No plates now exist on the Savage bridge—the fixing screws have all rusted away—but a photograph of the south portal, taken in 1923, shows just part of the top centre plate, with the letters '. . . LT BY B. & O. . . .' Careful examination, however, shows ghost outlines of all six plates clearly visible on both portals. The bridges built before 1866 had, on the evidence of photographs, no plates, and those built between then and 1870 have six, so it is a reasonable conclusion that the Savage bridge was made at some time after 1866 and before 1870. There consequently seems to be no reason to doubt the date of 1869, given in an anonymous memorandum in the Baltimore and Ohio archives.

Further detective work was required to discover, as a preliminary to restoration, the original colours in which the bridge was painted. The only evidence came from half a dozen wet-plate negatives of various Baltimore and Ohio bridges, taken in 1870–75, and from the assumption that the company, proud of its role as an innovator with iron bridges, would have wanted to show them off to visiting engineers from all over the world. A striking livery of some kind was therefore probable. The old photographs show what appears to be a consistent colour scheme, with the body of the bridge—the compressive elements—dark and heavy, and the main diagonals and counterstays—the tensile elements—light and airy. References to the shades of other items in the pictures, such as trees and cloth, and to certain known Victorian conventions, suggested that the light colour was a deep ivory and the dark colour a deep red. The caps on the end tower and certain panels were obviously white and caused no problems of interpretation.

The Savage bridge is an excellent illustration of the role which the imagination has to play in any successful interpretation of archaeological data. In this particular case, the bridge owes its survival and its preservation as a technological monument of great national importance to the lucky chance that its history was pieced together by someone possessing both considerable engineering knowledge and exceptional intuition. Without this fortunate combination of qualities in a person who also happened to be in a position of influence, the last example of one of America's most significant nineteenth-century engineering achievements would have gone for scrap ten years ago.

One of the questions which industrial archaeologists can do a great deal to answer is not so much 'What was this?', although this is useful, but 'Why is this important now, and how important was it in its own day?' If we visit Ironbridge, in Shropshire, for example, it is clear enough, when we stand by the river and look along the gorge, that we are looking at an elegant bridge with the roadway going up to a pointed hump in the middle. We know, or we are told, that its date is 1779 and that it was probably—it is well to be cautious in these matters—the first iron bridge anywhere in the world. But it is only if we ask, 'Why was it built here? Why was it made of iron and like this? What were the problems in making it?' that its true interest becomes apparent. This, we discover, was the most logical of all

OPPOSITE
Detail of the Iron
Bridge, Coalbrookdale,
showing the carpen-
tery-type construction.

places for the pioneering iron bridge to be. In the eighteenth century the River Severn was Britain's most important industrial highway. There were ironworks and coal-mines and factories close to both its banks, and at Coalbrookdale, close to the Iron Bridge, Abraham Darby had his famous furnaces where he pioneered the smelting of iron with coke. The fact that he carried out these successful experiments at Coalbrookdale was also no accident, since the local coal had the low sulphur content that the process demanded. Given the existence of the ironworks, given the need to bridge the Severn Gorge in order to establish an early through route between mines, ironworks and customers on both sides of the river, and, above all, given the Darbys, with their immense confidence in the possibilities of iron, the Iron Bridge was inevitable. It would have been a professional betrayal for the Darbys to have built it of any other material. But, as we can see from the structure of the bridge, their confidence had its limits. They were only adventurous up to a certain point. The iron ribs of the bridge are mortised and pegged together, exactly as if they were made of wood. Ten years later, bridge builders, including the Darbys themselves, had abandoned this pseudo-carpentering technique and were going the whole way with bridges made of complete cast-iron sections.

Canals, too, give rise to fundamental questions. Why did the British, who were so eager to build canals up to the time the railways were built, become defeatist and abandon them? Why, in contrast, did engineers in other countries, America, Canada, Belgium and Russia, decide to deepen and widen their first canals, to make them suitable for sea-going twentieth-century ships and giant barges? Did the British regard canals as permanently old-fashioned, outdated by railways? Was the railway lobby so strong and so persuasive that it was able to brainwash the Government, manufacturers and the public into believing that railways could transport every kind of merchandise more cheaply than any other method of transport? Or was it, as some economic historians believe, that the railways and the colonies between them mopped up such an enormous share of the nation's investment savings that there was little left for anything else? The most likely answer is that Britain's canal system was, with two exceptions—the Caledonian Canal and the Manchester Ship Canal—designed entirely for inland transport, and it was never envisaged that it could one day be possible and sensible to bring sea-going ships directly into the industrial areas, as a number of countries now do.

OPPOSITE
Excavation of Olive
Mount cutting, Liver-
pool, 1830.

This may well be the explanation of the Toytown nature of most of the British canals, but it is also the cause of their great charm and of their present suitability for pleasure-boating. Nobody in his right mind would want to spend a holiday on the Manchester Ship Canal or on the canal from Zeebrugge to Bruges, but nothing could be more pleasant than a few days on the Kennet and Avon in Berkshire and Wiltshire, which is commercially useless.

The Corinth Canal in Greece, completed as late as 1893, is also picturesque, in a more dramatic way, and also too narrow to be used by modern shipping, but it has considerable value as a tourist attraction, not least because of its remarkable history. It was begun by Nero in AD 67, with the aim of avoiding the laborious and time-consuming process of dragging ships overland from one side of the Isthmus of Corinth to the other. The labour force used by Nero's engineers consisted of 6,000 prisoners from Judaea. A large part of the excavation had been completed when the work was brought to an abrupt halt by the rebellion of Vindex in Gaul. The canal remained in that unfinished state for 1,800 years, when it was finished with the help of equipment somewhat more modern than was available to Nero's slaves. There have been few more expensive canals to build. Nine and a half of its sixteen kilometres had to be cut through solid rock, to a depth of 54.86 metres. It is not the sort of place or the sort of work a prisoner of war remembers with pleasure.

Until recently the human history of canals, as of railways, has been strangely ignored, and one day, no doubt, this will be put right by a new generation of historians who are as interested in people as in technology and finance. Few canals repay this sort of study, the how-and-by-whom method of writing history, more than the Rideau Canal, in Ontario.

The Canadian canals were largely financed by the British Government, at first for military reasons, to transport men and munitions to the interior of the country. The plan was to make the St Lawrence navigable throughout its length and to provide a through route from Lake Erie to Lake Ontario and then to the St Lawrence and the sea. The Rideau Canal, or as it is really, the canalised Rideau River, was opened to traffic in 1834, and was an important link in the waterway chain from Lake Erie to the sea. It served little economic purpose—canals on the United States side of the border, and then railways, brought inland freight to the Atlantic ports more quickly—but it is one of the most beautiful of all the inland waterways of North America and understandably popular with holidaymakers during

Above Machinery at
Chaffey's Lock on the
Rideau Canal.
Below South Street,
New York City.

the summer months. Chaffey's Lock, where the canal runs into the oddly-named Lake Opinicon, is particularly interesting and agreeable. Here, a former mill has been converted into a hotel, and there are lawns leading down the slope to the locks where, according to taste, one can watch the launches and canoes coming through or admire the splendid workmanship of the walls of the lock, which are finished to the highest standards. How craftsmen of this degree of skill were persuaded or bribed to come to such a remote and, at that time, disease-ridden spot remains a mystery. The locks have been well maintained and the whole length of 197 kilometres is navigable. Few, if any, of the early nineteenth-century canals on either side of the Atlantic are in such excellent repair or so little altered. If there can be such a thing as archaeology in perfect condition, this is it, and its very completeness compels the historian to turn his energies in other directions, to discover all he can about the building of the canal and about the activities which went on along the route when freight and passenger boats were passing all the time from April until November.

The Rideau was built under contract, the work being supervised by officers of the Royal Engineers, led by the legendary Colonel John By. Most of the country through which it ran contained no settlements at all, so that horses and oxen were very difficult to obtain. It was easier to get men than draught animals—Irish labourers were brought in by the shipload—so wheelbarrows were the normal form of transport. The Irish labourers were completely inexperienced and exceptionally accident-prone, especially where explosives were concerned. Many of them died of a particularly virulent form of malaria, known as swamp fever, or canal fever. On one occasion, in 1828 at Jones Falls, there was nobody in the camp capable of taking even a drink to a sick man, since everyone, the doctor included, was ill with the disease.

The archaeology of the Rideau must certainly include the cemeteries dotted along the route. Cemeteries are an unnecessarily neglected and very fruitful aspect of industrial archaeology; one can learn a lot from them. These cemeteries are, unfortunately, badly neglected. One of them, known as McGuigan's Cemetery, is near Nicholson's Locks. To reach it, one goes through an orchard adjoining the main road and there, by the side of the canal, is a much overgrown hillock, with gravestones all over it, some still upright, but the majority toppled over and half-covered with grass and bushes. A number of the men who built the canal and who died of

McGuigan's Cemetery on the Rideau Canal.

fever are buried here, together with a number of the early settlers. One stone has a child's head carved on it, commemorating a little girl who was drowned in Clowes Lock while it was being constructed. On either side of it are the graves of her parents, both fever victims, who died soon afterwards.

The Women's Institutes of Canada have an excellent institution, known as the Tweedsmuir Books, in which individual Institutes collect their members' memories of life in the district as it used to be. One such entry, from Newboro Institute, recalls the old days of the Rideau. This lady remembers tugs

'. . . towing two, three and four barges; about forty sailing scows carried out wood, lumber, pressed hay, grain, horses, cheese, whatever the country had to sell, and brought in goods the merchants sold, the implements that were needed, the foodstuffs not grown in this climate, and furnished employment to hundreds of men. Rafts of squared timber and of rough logs running up to hundreds of lock bands, built up with cook- and bunk-houses, made their slow way to mills and market every year and left behind a fire menace. I have seen the men at Jones Falls at work without a break for over sixty hours. They slept on the grass while the locks were filling and ate their meals that had been brought to them sitting on a swing bar. They worked twenty-four hours a day and slept when they could. At first the lock men were paid sixty cents a day for seven and a half months each year. Later their pay was raised to a dollar a day, and there never was any trouble in getting men to work on the lock.'

With this kind of information available, the locks on the Rideau are no longer dead constructions of stone, wood and iron. They are waterway equipment operated by men who worked sixty hours at a stretch for a dollar a day. And they were built by men who came from Ireland, died of canal fever and lie buried in forgotten places like McGuigan's Cemetery.

To appreciate its history and its technical achievement, a canal has to be thought of as a unit. The archaeology of a canal is the canal as a whole, not a flight of locks here and a viaduct or pumping station there; and one can never get the feeling of it in its working days merely by driving to one or two points on it and standing on the tow-path. The essential feature of a canal was, and is, its slow pace, and to appreciate this one must either walk along it or go the way the traffic used to, by boat. Seen from the canal, the buildings and installations by the side of it make sense, they are integrated with it and in the right proportions; but approached, as they usually are, in a car that turns off a modern main road, they can seem absurdly small and amateurish.

The Kennet and Avon is a satisfying, if sad, canal to explore, satisfying because of the variety and peacefulness of the countryside it runs through, but sad because it had such a short life and so much of it is derelict, with lock-gates rotted away, considerable stretches dry, weeds uncut and tow-paths overgrown with bushes. Here the imagination has to work rather harder than it does on the Rideau, since it is so much more decayed.

There are two methods of studying the Kennet and Avon. One is to think of it as a waterway—the pleasure-boaters' approach—and the other as a succession of tourist-worthy, scholar-worthy landmarks. These landmarks certainly exist—the pumping stations at Claverton and Crofton, the former canal company offices at Bath, the Dundas aqueduct—but they are not, by themselves, the archaeology of the Kennet and Avon. The archaeology is the clay lining which stopped the canal from leaking, where the soil, as in the Bath area, is naturally porous, and the paths leading down from the tow-path from time to time, so that the horses could have a rest in a convenient meadow, just as much as it is the stone of the Avoncliff viaduct and the iron and steam of the Crofton Pumping Station. One can, in other words, choose to think of the canal either as a single continuous site—the ecological and more meaningful method—or, more conventionally, as a series of sites. But, whichever point of view one adopts, it is impossible not to be impressed by the remarkable chain of twenty-nine locks through Devizes, the second longest flight in Britain, closely rivalling the thirty at Tandebigge on the Worcester and Birmingham Canal.

The locks are built along a stretch of more than four kilometres, with seventeen in a straight line, 22·86 metres apart and with a rise of 2·43 metres each. All twenty-nine of the locks are 22·5 metres long, with a flotation depth of 1·22 metres. They could accommodate barges up to 4·26 metres wide. Each lock had to have its own individual reservoir, to supply sufficient water when the traffic was heavy. The whole flight lifts the canal 72·85 metres between Semington and Devizes, and under average conditions a barge could go from one end to the other in three hours. This meant two things; the lock-keeper had to work exceedingly hard, night and day, and the number of barges which could pass along the canal in twenty-four hours depended entirely on the system of getting traffic through these locks. Devizes was a bottleneck. If this unfortunate seventy-two-metre rise had not existed, more barges could have been moved between Reading and Bath.

The only way of really seeing the Devizes locks and of giving proper credit to this remarkable engineering achievement is to fly over the area in a helicopter. One then understands what a formidable task it was, to terrace a long hillside with more or less waterproof basins, and to do this with spade-and-wheelbarrow labour, and one sees what an expensive problem it is going to be to get this water-staircase back into operation again, as the Kennet and Avon Trust says it has every intention of doing. The locks have all fallen in, with the collapse of the gates and the pressure of water and mud from above, and, viewed from the air, what was once the pride and

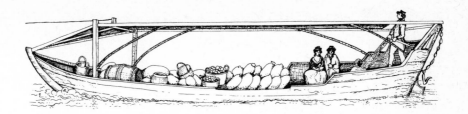

The Market or Passage Boat, from a print of 1796.

joy of its engineer, John Rennie, now looks not unlike a series of bomb craters.

The British Waterways Museum at Stoke Bruerne, in Northamptonshire, falls into two parts, an indoor section housed in the former canal warehouse, and a number of barges moored near the lock outside; which is a sensible way of bringing archaeology alive. A similar idea, buildings plus boats, has been applied at a number of seaports around the world. The most ambitious, and on the whole the most successful, is at Mystic, Connecticut. Not everyone who sees it comes away entirely satisfied, but since all conversations about maritime archaeology eventually come round to Mystic, it is as well to know what has been attempted and accomplished there.

Mystic owes its existence to shipbuilding and whaling. Between 1838 and 1878 Greenman's yard—the largest—launched nearly a hundred ships of all kinds, from small sloops to the famous clipper, *David Crockett*, whose average time over twenty-five runs round Cape Horn to San Francisco was never equalled. By 1840 Mystic had become important as a whaling port, and when whaling was at its height, in 1845, the local shipowners had eighteen of these ships. With the California gold rush the yards turned their attention to building clipper ships, and built twenty-two of them. During the Civil War fifty-six troop transports and other steamships were produced here. The Mystic shipbuilders formed their own engineering company and manufactured steam-engines not only for their own ships, but also for steamships constructed elsewhere. Nowadays building is confined to yachts and fishing boats.

The museum, known as Mystic Seaport, is not the old town of Mystic at all, most of which has been burned or pulled down over the years. What visitors see, and Mystic is one of the most popular museums in the United States, is an excellent collection of old buildings with maritime associations which have been brought from elsewhere. There is a workshop which made mast hoops, a clock shop, a tavern, a seamen's chapel, a rigging loft, a rope-walk, a ship's chandlery, and so on. To these are added a large collection of

Mystic Seaport.

ships of all sizes, the centrepiece being the wooden whaling ship, *Charles W. Morgan*, built in 1841 at the yard of Jethro and Zacharial Hillman, in New Bedford, Massachusetts.

All these are excellent museum pieces, and it is fortunate that they have been saved from destruction, but they have nothing directly to do with Mystic. They are antiques, not archaeology. Mystic is a synthetic seaport. In fact, almost the only buildings there which can truly be said to relate to the archaeology of Mystic are the three houses which once belonged to members of the Greenman family, the port's leading shipbuilders. These houses, built between 1839 and 1842 when the family fortunes were at their peak, illustrate very well the standard of living achieved by prosperous manufacturers at this time. Like the managers' and directors' houses at the Sura-hammar Ironworks in Sweden, they are large and comfortable, without being in any way ostentatious or mansion-like, very different from the vulgar palaces which rich businessmen began to build for themselves in America after the Civil War.

To compare the Greenman family houses at Mystic or the du Pont house at the Eleutherian Mills with, say, Biltmore in North Carolina, completed for George W. Vanderbilt in 1895, is to realise the transformation which took place in the scale of American industry, and in the fortunes to be made from it, during the second half of the last century. The Vanderbilts' money came from railways and shipping. Biltmore was just one of their mansions. It was situated in an estate of 125,000 acres and it had 250 rooms. A temporary five-kilometre railway spur line had to be built to carry construction materials to the site. In addition to the hundreds of workmen from the area, skilled craftsmen from all over the United States and from many parts of Europe came to cut and fit the Indiana limestone and to carry out the elaborate carving required. More than a thousand workers were steadily busy for five years before the house was ready. The world was ransacked for furniture and art treasures to fit out the 250 rooms and the gardens and park were laid out by Frederick Law Olmsted, who landscaped Central Park in New York.

Biltmore's size made it a little out of the ordinary, even in the United States, but many industrial magnates achieved a similar level of grandeur and often absurdity for themselves. They built palaces, not houses, and they are best regarded as princes or, as they became known in America itself, robber-barons. Their palaces are an important part of the industrial archaeology of America, and so, too, are the less extravagant houses of their predecessors, people like the Greenmans. One of the Greenman houses is open to the public. It has been furnished in the mid-Victorian style, with a few original Greenman pieces and several family portraits.

The contrast between Mystic and another American maritime museum, at South Street, New York City, is very marked. Here, too, is a collection of old ships, but those chosen for preservation and display at South Street all have a close connexion with the port and trade of New York. The buildings are the original quayside buildings, the fish market, the taverns, the chandlers, the shops of various kinds, rescued and preserved as a whole, to give visitors something of the atmosphere of this part of Manhattan when everything was still on a human scale. The contrast between the two- and three-storeyed buildings of the South Street area and the skyscrapers towering up immediately behind it is very marked, a reminder of the gulf that exists between the old America of craftsmen and small businessmen and the new America of giant corporations. The deserted quays and piers on the other side of Manhattan, once crowded with transatlantic liners and their passengers, and now replaced by the aeroplane, make the same point.

Little harbours, with their eighteenth- and nineteenth-century quays and buildings, have remarkable stamina, but for the big ports —Rotterdam, New Orleans, Southampton, Le Havre, Hamburg,

St Katharine's Dock, showing the nineteenth-century centre of the European ivory trade, the vaults of which once housed convicts awaiting transportation to Australia.

Antwerp, Montreal—the motto since 1945 has been 'Modernise or die'. The slaughter of old warehouses and other port installations has been on a massive scale, some through wartime bombing—ports are always favourite targets—and some through clearance and rebuilding. Sometimes an unusually imaginative piece of planning has made it possible to incorporate some of the old buildings in a new development scheme. This has been done at Liverpool, where it is proposed that the magnificent Albert Dock warehouses should be converted into premises for Liverpool Polytechnic; in Copenhagen, where a large warehouse is now a restaurant and hotel; and at the St Katharine's Dock, near the Tower of London, where part of the complex designed by Thomas Telford and Philip Hardwick in the 1820s has been converted to expensive flats, sharing a view of the dock and the river with the World Trade Centre and the 826-room Tower Hotel. A small collection of old ships serves as a reminder of the days when the Dock earned a maritime living.

Other ports have been less fortunate in preserving tangible

remains of their history. In Bergen a series of mysterious fires have destroyed numbers of the beautiful timber warehouses which gave the waterfront its special character and charm. In Marseilles, much of the old port was blown up during the Second World War, and in Bristol the closing of the City Docks has given a large part of the river area a regrettably down-at-heel appearance. But in all countries the difficulty of preserving even parts of ports and harbours as they were fifty or a hundred years ago is very great. The layouts required by container ships and bulk-carriers are not the same as those which dealt efficiently with the cargo ships and passenger liners of the late nineteenth century. Modern ships need a lot more land behind the dockside, for stacking and handling containers, for parking lorries and for temporary warehousing. The old buildings have to go, to provide these empty spaces. Any which are still there ten years from now will be rare accidents.

The process has happened before, of course. At the height of its prosperity, Kinsale, in Ireland's County Cork, was one of the chief ports of the British Navy, but the docks and quays were too small to accommodate the bigger ships of the later eighteenth century or the expansion of the shipbuilding industry. The Navy went elsewhere, but the harbour (now given over to yachts and fishing-boats) and the decaying warehouses bear witness to the town's former maritime prosperity. Naval dockyards, being more conservative, usually preserve their archaeology more successfully than commercial ports. At Portsmouth, for example, many of the dockyard buildings date from the mid-eighteenth century. They include a number of fine, brick-built storehouses, of which Numbers 11, 12 and 18 are the best architecturally; the building—but not, alas, the equipment—of a large rope-walk; and the late eighteenth-century block-making shop, with its original machine-body, designed by Maudslay and Marc Brunel. In the Royal Dockyard, Copenhagen, one can still see a number of eighteenth-century warehouses and the wooden crane (1784), fixed to the top of a square brick tower, which was used to step and unstep ships' masts.

Old airports have mostly gone the way of old seaports. Most of the airports of the 1920s and '30s were fairly close to the centres of the cities they served. They did not need long runways, because the aeroplanes that used them were small, and their terminal buildings could be of modest size, because they had to handle very few passengers. The only major airport of the pre-Second World War period to survive much as it was is Tempelhof, in West Berlin, and

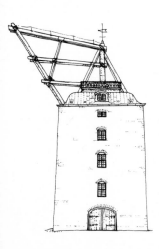

Crane at the Royal Dockyard, Copenhagen.

we shall not see this a great deal longer. Tempelhof, by today's standards, is quite inadequate. It is ringed with housing estates and it cannot take large aircraft. But, from a passenger's point of view, it is exceedingly convenient. It is close to the city—almost part of it, in fact; and one has only a very short distance to walk to one's plane, and luggage arrives remarkably quickly. Pre-war passengers took such things for granted, but nowadays they seem a marvellous luxury. The generation of airports to which Tempelhof, Croydon and Le Bourget belonged gave excellent service to the privileged élite who used them. They were not built to deal with tens of thousands of people each day, but those who had the money and the courage to go by air had little to complain about.

Le Bourget, the only Paris airport until long after the 1939–45 war, is soon to close, but meanwhile its buildings are not greatly different from what they were half a century ago, although the amenities have changed somewhat. The aim at Le Bourget, as at Croydon, was to provide passengers with conditions not inferior to those they were accustomed to at the Gare de Lyon or Victoria. Waiting accommodation was on the first floor where in the words of the 1926 *Guide to Le Bourget Airport*, 'there is a very fine view over the airport'. There was a waiting-room, bureau de change, post and telegraph office and a range of telephone kiosks. In addition, 'as at railway stations', there was a bookstall. Since then—Le Bourget dates from the mid-twenties—there have been a few concessions to mass travel; mechanical baggage handling, a public-address system, a snack bar and, something the 1920s would have found difficulty in comprehending, a duty-free shop, together with car parks and security checks. But the buildings are as uncomplicated and as easy to find one's way about in as ever, and the distance from lounge to aeroplane is blissfully short.

On the way from London to Gatwick by road one passes the terminal building of what used to be Croydon Airport. The old airfield is now an industrial estate and there is little glamour about the terminal itself, which road-widening has brought very close to the highway outside. The new buildings at Croydon Airport, paid for by the Air Ministry, opened in 1928. 'On entering the domed booking hall,' said an air-line advertisement, 'one realises that air services have now taken their place in the civilised world as a recognised means of transport, no longer limited to a few adventurous spirits, but used daily by business men as well as those travelling for pleasure.' In London, there was a city terminal in Charles Street, off

Arriving at the new
Croydon Airport, 1928.

Berkeley Square, if one was travelling Imperial Airways, or in the Haymarket if the French line, Air Union, was chosen. Passengers and their baggage were weighed there and then taken in a small bus to Croydon. At Le Bourget, transport to Paris was by special bus or by tram. The New York City terminal, built in the 1930s, is still there, opposite Grand Central Station.

During the past twenty years a common practice in many countries has been, so to speak, to turn the airfield round, by abandoning the old terminal building and constructing a new one on another side of the airfield. This has been done, for example, at Dublin and Schiphol (Amsterdam) and provides an excellent opportunity to compare the old and the new, and especially their relative size. Where there is no room to enlarge an airfield, to allow it to take modern aircraft, there is no point in putting up new terminal buildings, and the airport has to be abandoned. One of the most curious results of this can be seen in Bristol. The original airport there, in service until the 1950s, was on the south side of the city, at Whitchurch. This has now been built over, but the existence of Whit-

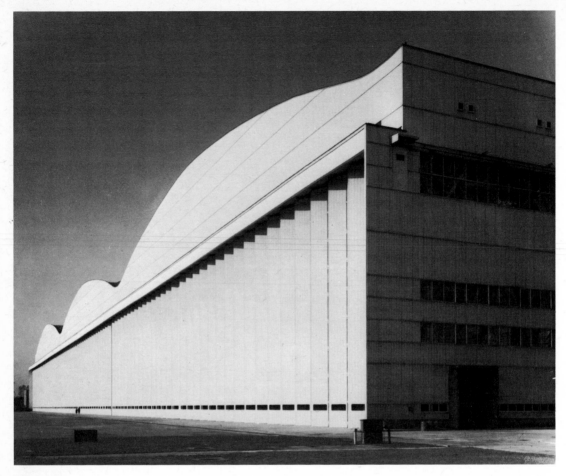

Folding doors at
the Brabazon Assembly
Hall, Filton, Bristol.

church Airport is commemorated by a public house nearby, which
has an aeroplane on its sign, and the name, now a mere piece of
folklore, *Happy Landings*.

There are old items of aviation archaeology to be observed in
many places. Some are obvious, some less so. At Hucclecote, outside
Gloucester, for instance, the elegant modern facade of the ICI Fibres
plant masks the front of what was once the Gloster Aircraft Co.,
closed down in the 1950s, when fighter aircraft were no longer
required, and converted to the manufacture of nylon yarn. At
Calshot Spit, easily seen from the boat that goes between Southampton and the Isle of Wight, one can still see the slipways and some of
the buildings used by Imperial Airways' famous pre-war flying-boat
service.

These, however, are very small affairs by comparison with the airship hangars at Cardington, Bedfordshire. Both are 47·5 metres long.
The first was built in 1917 and extended in 1927, at the time of the

construction of the R100 and R101. The second hangar was added in 1927, the year of the R101's maiden flight. The R101 broke her back, caught fire and crashed at the beginning of a flight to India and the R100 was broken up for scrap soon afterwards. The Cardington hangars remain as a memorial to them both, the last passenger-carrying airships ever built in Britain.

Bristol has a distinguished monument at Filton to another aviation folly, the *Brabazon* airliner. A huge assembly hall was needed to build the prototype of this expensive aeroplane that never went into production. The enormous doors, 20 metres high and with thirty-two folding leaves, and a total of 318·5 metres long, had to be made of aluminium if they were to be moved at all. They weigh 200 tons, and can be opened in two minutes flat. Few people now remember the *Brabazon*, which went the way of so many aircraft projects, but its hangar is still there, earning a useful living as a base for over-hauling more recent BAC aircraft.

5

The Food and Drink Industries

In 1906 the American novelist and social reformer, Upton Sinclair, published a book about a family of immigrants who worked in Chicago's stockyards and packing factories. It was called *The Jungle*, and with its spare-nothing exposure of the conditions under which America's meat was produced, it soon became a best-seller. At the beginning of the book, a party of visitors is taken round the yards and factories.

> 'There is over a square mile of space in the yards,' they learnt, 'and more than half of it is occupied by cattle pens; north and south as far as the eye can see there stretches a sea of pens. And they were all filled—so many cattle no one had ever dreamed existed in the world.'

To move all these animals in alive and out dead was a formidable problem.

> 'There were two hundred and fifty miles of track within the yards,' their guide went on to tell them. 'They brought about ten thousand head of cattle every day, and as many hogs, and half as many sheep—which meant some eight or ten million live creatures turned into food every year.'

All this was made possible by the railway, which allowed the ranchers and farmers to get their cattle quickly from the rail-heads at Dodge City, Ellsworth and Abilene to the meat-packing factories in Chicago and Kansas City. 'Packing' meant converting an animal into every possible saleable product, from canned beef, sausage and hides to glue and bone-meal. The more steers and pigs and sheep

Looking west on
Exchange Avenue,
Union Stockyard *c.*
1905.

that could be brought to one central place, the easier it was to have
the soap factories, the candle factories, the lard factories, the fertiliser factories and the can-making factories all conveniently close to
one another, with the economies that large-scale production made
possible. Before the days of refrigeration, the meat itself had to be
preserved in some way, canned or salted or smoked, if it was to reach
its customers in the Eastern States or on the other side of the Atlantic
in an edible condition. The more processes a company controlled
itself, the bigger its profits were likely to be. Armours, Swifts and the
other great meat-packing companies were not in Chicago for the
health of their proprietors.

Today, nearly seventy years after the publication of Upton
Sinclair's book, the stockyards and the packing factories have gone.
The meat is dealt with in smaller and more salubrious places all over
the United States, wherever the cattle are raised, and Chicago is not
altogether sorry. The image of the city created by *The Jungle* on the
one hand and bootleggers and gangsters on the other is one which is
better changed, and not much sympathy has been available for
anyone who has suggested that a section of the stockyards should be
preserved for posterity to look at, with maybe a museum of meat-

OPPOSITE
Galleria Vittorio
Emmanuele, Milan.

packing for old time's sake. Anyone visiting the site now will see a fair amount of dereliction and abandoned buildings; railway sidings not yet removed; the great entrance gateway to the Union Stockyards, which is to be preserved as a historic monument; one or two of the drinking places frequented by the slaughter-men; and, within the district, a fair number of slums, the former homes of the packing-plant employees, which have not yet been pulled down and replaced. This is the archaeology of meat-packing. The area is now dead, with no smells, no masses of negroes and immigrants rushing to and from work, no cattle trains, no auctioneers. Within ten years, the entrance gateway will be largely meaningless, marooned among new housing estates and factories.

Slaughterhouses and their equipment are among the items of industrial archaeology which are least likely to be preserved, but for some countries, such as Denmark, they have played an important part in the economy and export trade of the country during the past century. Without slaughterhouses and curing-rooms, there would have been no Danish bacon, but nobody has seen fit to preserve any of the early buildings and equipment connected with this industry.

The dairying industry, however, has faired better, despite the fact that commercial competition and increasingly strict public health regulations have long since made the nineteenth- and early twentieth-century milk- and meat-processing factories obsolete and, indeed, illegal, and little survives of their equipment outside museums. However, one of Denmark's earliest milk factories, at Mandø (1897) was transferred in 1958 to the open-air agricultural museum at Hjerl Hede, in Jutland. It is a house-sized building, with a steam-engine to drive the machinery, which is in working order, but not original. The plant is operated for a short period each summer. Another old milk factory has, however, been preserved on its original site, at Ølgod, in West Jutland. Opened in 1882, it was Denmark's first commercial milk-processing factory. It was restored in 1950, using the original machinery.

So long as the rural economy was organised on the basis of poor transport between one district and another, every country had its local flour mills, slaughterhouses and breweries and its parish-by-parish system for marketing dairy produce. It was only the coming of the canals and railways which made it possible for these processing units to be enlarged to the point at which they could be called industries. In England, the growth in scale of the brewing and food industries during the nineteenth century was due mainly to a wish

Milk-processing factory at Ølgod, West Jutland, Denmark, 1882.

Above Covent Garden by the Victorian artist, Phoebus Levin, 1864. *Below* Coalbrookdale at night, as seen by the artist P. J. de Loutherbourg, *c.* 1800.

to sell to the profitable and rapidly expanding London market. The first wholesale milk depot to be established primarily to meet the demands of London was opened at Semley in Wiltshire, in 1871. It was built, logically, by the side of the Exeter–Waterloo railway line, and it is still operating. Two years later the Anglo-Swiss Company (it is now Nestlés) opened Wiltshire's pioneering milk-processing factory at Chippenham in a disused cloth mill. A similar change of use occurred in 1897 nearby at Staverton. In this case, Nestlés took over a large woollen mill, dating from about 1810, and converted it fairly ruthlessly, demolishing its top two storeys and adding new buildings. The break between cloth and butter was never complete, however. A steam-engine which was operating at Staverton in 1831 continued working there until 1945.

These milk depots and factories, belonging nowadays to one of the three big groups, Unigate, Express Dairies and Nestlés, were set up to take advantage of the railway network. A survey of them now, with many of the branch lines gone, shows how strategically placed these depots were. They are closest together where the cows are thickest on the ground, built where the milk could be brought in by horse and cart without making such a journey unreasonably long. During the past twenty years many of these creameries, such as Bason Bridge in Somerset, and Bailey Gate in Dorset, have found themselves deprived of the railway which made their existence possible in the first place. Many have been closed down and are used for other purposes. The collecting depot at Castle Cary in Somerset, for instance, is now a re-treading factory for lorry and tractor tyres, and the one at Frome belongs to a firm of builders' merchants. These local centres for receiving churns of milk, tipping the milk into railway tank-wagons and steam-sterilising the churns for return to the farms, made sense only as long as milk arrived by horse and cart. Once lorry transport became normal, the depots could be much further apart and the milk could be taken straight to London by road. The railway gradually became irrelevant.

One can see much the same change operating with beer. Throughout the beer-drinking world, the number of breweries has been declining steadily during the present century, with production concentrated into a very few large units. The process is well illustrated by what happened to a medium-sized brewery at Wiveliscombe, in Somerset. This brewery, which had its own maltings, was established early in the nineteenth century and owned a number of public houses in Somerset. In 1958 it was bought by a large brewery company in Trowbridge, closed, and sold to a firm producing broiler chickens. Within two years, the Trowbridge-based company was taken over by an even larger concern and finally, in 1972, this company in turn was absorbed into a mammoth group. Brewing has now ceased in Trowbridge. The archaeology of all these changes and mergers has consequently become very complicated. It includes a broiler-chicken plant in Trowbridge, together with the mansion of the original brewing family, now converted into flats; a large number of public houses; an ex-brewery in Trowbridge, together with its public houses; and the breweries, maltings, offices and public houses belonging to the two London-based take-over firms. The merger and the system of large centralised production units which resulted from them killed the traditional brewing process, in which nothing but malt and hops was used, pasteurisation was not dreamt of, and the beer was allowed to mature quietly and naturally before being drunk.

In America, one can say with some confidence that no old breweries survive. In Europe, they can be counted almost on the fingers of one hand. In England there is a flourishing example at Hook Norton, in north Oxfordshire, where the now almost vanished tower-system is followed, the brewing process being started at the top of the tower and finishing down at the bottom. This brewery smells of brewing, a phenomenon which has become almost as rare as the sound of a crowing cock. A number of old-style breweries have been preserved but, since they no longer function, they have lost an essential dimension, the smell of the mash-tun and the brewing copper.

The oldest brewery in the world which is still operating is probably the former Royal Brewhouse at Schwarzach in Bavaria. The building dates from 1689 and is a curious example of the baroque concept of how an industrial building should look. Two-storeyed, with round-arched windows, it looks not unlike a church. The original brewing equipment disappeared a long time ago and what is now in use is part nineteenth-, part twentieth-century.

A brewery of the old type has been reconstructed at the open-air museum at Bokrijk, near Hasselt in Belgium. The early eighteenth-century building comes from the village of Diepenbeek, near Hasselt. In the old days the brewery at Diepenbeek was run as a monopoly by the local squire. During the French Revolution, the monopoly was abolished and the brewery became a house. In 1954 it was given to the museum, and rebuilt stone by stone. In it was installed the village brewery from Hougaerde near Louvain, which has surviving inventories and other records from the middle of the eighteenth century. The equipment includes a mash-tun, a wooden fermentation vat, a copper wort-boiler. There is a row of casks for transporting the beer, with tubs underneath to catch the yeast as it was ejected from the brew. After five or six days in the casks, the ale was fined with isinglass and drawn off into stone jars. The final fermentation was carried out at the tavern or in the customer's house.

Other small breweries transferred to museums include the eighteenth-century malt and kiln house from Trosa, in Sweden, which now forms part of the Brewing Museum in Stockholm; the mid-nineteenth-century 'white beer' brewery—a compound of elements from several breweries—at the open-air museum at Åarhus, in Jutland; and the eighteenth-century village brewery, *De Roskam* (the Curry Comb) from North Brabant, in the Netherlands, now re-erected at the open-air museum at Arnhem. These little breweries, entirely typical of their period, aimed only at providing for the needs of their immediate locality; and the quality of the beer they brewed was exceedingly variable, just as no two cooks produce meals of the same quality. The contrast between them and Whitbread's late eighteenth-century porter brewery—a vast building for the time—in Chiswell Street, London, is very striking. Whitbread's had the great London market on their doorstep, together with the ships in the Port of London, which needed provisioning for their voyages. To meet this demand it was worthwhile, as it was for similar reasons in the Portsmouth and Chatham areas, to invest in a big plant, and for many years, Chiswell Street, where the main brewing hall is still preserved, was one of the wonders of the brewing world. Many visitors came to see it each year, and to admire its ingenious machinery for moving the grain and malt from floor to floor.

Most of the great nineteenth-century city breweries, like Watney's Stag's Head Brewery, near Victoria Station, in London, have now been demolished—their sites were too valuable for mere brewing— or adapted and modernised out of all recognition. In Amsterdam, for example, the Amstel Brewery, which was established on its present site in 1870, has few traces of the original buildings. Copenhagen has rather more to offer. In the middle of the nineteenth century a new type of beer was developed in the Pilsen area of what is now Czechoslovakia. It was what brewers called a bottom-fermented beer, light in colour, with a slightly bitter taste of hops and sparkling from the chemist's addition of carbon dioxide, a very different drink from the traditional dark, top-fermented beer which Europeans had been drinking since the Middle Ages. The Tuborg Brewery in Copenhagen produced the new, Pilsen-type beer from the time the brewery first started operating, in 1873, but the Tuborg plant today is a very modern affair. Its premises, one of the prominent features of Copenhagen's waterfront, date only from 1945. The King's Brew House, however, which now belongs to the Tuborg group, is still, externally, much as it was last century, a pleasant little building in the old part of the city. The other great Copenhagen brewing firm, Carlsberg, preserves much of the nineteenth-century atmosphere, despite major additions in recent years. Its Brewery Museum, with very Victorian collections of sculpture, paintings and documents, is as much a monument to the founders, Carl and Ottilia Jacobsen, as it is to brewing. The flavour of paternalism, and of the Victorian virtues of charity, piety and patriotism, is somewhat overwhelming. The formidable gatehouse, supported by giant granite elephants, and with its motto, *Laboremus Pro Patria* (Let us toil for the Father-land), was no doubt intended to inspire the workers to greater efforts as they passed through it on their way in to work in the morn-

Entrance portico to the Carlsberg Brewery, Copenhagen.

ing, but it is, at the same time, a splendid symbol of the spirit and reality of a successful nineteenth-century family business.

To the Irish, beer traditionally means Guinness, and the archaeology of Guinness is of considerable interest. The first Arthur Guinness began brewing at St James's Gate in 1759 and for two hundred years the firm was Dublin's main employer, with its own fleet of ships to bring barley and hops almost to the door and to take the beer down the Liffey over the sea to Britain. Latterly, the demand for Guinness has fallen off, both in England and in Ireland, with the growing fashion for something lighter and supposedly less fattening, and the great St James's brewery is much contracted. Large parts of it have been demolished, but enough remains to serve as a reminder of the days when Guinness was Dublin. Fortunately, as the brewery has been tailored down to a size better suited to the 1970s, the excellent Guinness Museum, set up in 1968 in the old Research Laboratory buildings, has been able to provide a home for some of the old equipment and historical material which has had to be discarded. Here in the museum are displays illustrating the technical and commercial development of the firm, with collections

Early nineteenth-
century wine-press,
from the Champagne
Museum, Épernay.

of tools, machines, bottles, labels and, fortunately, its unrivalled advertisements.

During the past twenty years, the casualty rate among old breweries has been higher than for any other category of building (including railway stations) of interest to the industrial archaeologist. Many breweries are architecturally very attractive and, since brewing was not a poor industry, they were well built. They deserve, and do not always get, careful recording. So for that matter do the brewers' outlets, public houses, which are constantly having their appearance and interior arrangements changed by modernisation and extension. A few survive in their more or less primitive condition, especially in Ireland—there is a superb example of a nineteenth-century stand-up-and-drink saloon at Maynooth, near Dublin, a stone's throw from the great theological college and complete with partitions to localise fights and quarrels. Drinking-places are as much a part of the brewery industry as garages and filling-stations are of the motor industry, and they deserve proper attention from historians and archaeologists.

The wine industry, like brewing, has undergone great changes during the past half-century. The general tendency has been towards larger and larger producing, fermenting, storage and bottling units and away from the picturesque cellars and presses which one would still like to consider typical of what has been a craft-and-mystique industry for so long. The aim nowadays, however, seems to be to get as close as possible to the Australian methods of production, with huge vineyards, tractor cultivation and bulk shipment, which has proved so successful that the Australians can land wine in Europe cheaper than the French, Germans or Italians can make it themselves.

One sees this process of industrialisation operating to a very marked extent in Yugoslavia, which is an important wine-producing country. Since the end of the war in 1945, large new plants have been built, especially in the Dubrovnik area, to replace the old peasant-type structures. Some of these buildings, at Vršac and Gruda, for instance, are excellent examples of modern industrial architecture. The old type of cellarage, above ground and looking rather like old fire-station buildings, without doors, can be seen at Topola and Potmoje. At Maribor there are fine vaulted cellars, which contain monumental storage casks, similar to those which can be found in the Trentino district of Italy and, of course, at Heidelberg.

Portugal, which is a low-wage country and for this reason better able to continue with methods using a great deal of labour, has not as yet gone very far along the modernisation trail in its wine industry and many interesting monuments survive. Vila Nova da Gaia, the Roman Cale, is the main storage centre for wines from the Upper Douro, the so-called port wines. The new wine is brought in casks to the wine lodges at Vila Nova in April, and left there for maturing, blending and eventual shipment abroad. The port wine lodges mostly date from the late eighteenth century, and are pleasant, whitewashed buildings, with arched colonnades along the front. The great pipes of port are stacked inside, up to four high. Coimbra, too, has a number of important wine lodges. In Oporto itself, the commercial centre of the wine industry, the British Factory House (1785) illustrates the long and close links between England, traditionally the great port-drinking nation, and Portugal. The Factory House, whose members were drawn from the numerous port wine firms, was a combination of club, exchange and depot.

Wine links with Britain are also very strong and old-established in Spain. Jerez, the centre of the sherry trade, has been the headquarters of a number of large shippers and merchants for many generations. Chief among these firms are Gonzalez Byass, and

A Jerez bodega.

Williams and Humbert, both of whom occupy pleasant eighteenth-century buildings. Jerez has a number of open-fronted bodegas—storehouses for wine—which have been in continuous use for more than two hundred years, and so, too, has Tarragona. Outside the sherry-producing area, there are some enormous cellars, among which those at San Sadurni de Noya, near Barcelona, are a well-known tourist attraction. The wine firm, Torres of Villafranca, has some of the oldest cellars in the region, with enormous wooden vats, one of which is reputed to hold half a million litres.

The archaeology of the food and drink industries can easily get out of hand, in the sense that one becomes too interested in the details and loses the economic and social patterns into which

Wine vat at the Champagne Museum, Épernay.

the individual items fit. One can, for instance, visit Gouda, in the Netherlands, and watch cheese being weighed and sold at the picturesque old cheese weigh-house, which has been used for the purpose since 1668. One can admire the wonderful collection of old wine-presses at Épernay, in the champagne area of France, or the rich variety of pasta at the Spaghetti Museum at Oneglia. These things are fascinating in themselves, and everyone is certainly better for seeing them. But to get full value from them, one has to have the curiosity and the courage to ask the kind of questions the guide books rarely mention. Why is Dutch cheese so remarkably tasteless, compared with English or French? Did the Dutch like it that way? Was it easier and more reliable to produce? Or was the Dutch type of cheese easier to roll on to barges and bring down the canals? How big an area did the cheese markets and weigh-houses at Gouda and Alkmaar serve? Why did and do the Italians eat so much pasta? Do they really like it in such prodigious quantities, or do they buy it because they are too poor to buy anything better? Is there any connexion between pasta-eating and the deplorable shape of most Italians over the age of twenty-five or thirty?

If one could take a God's-eye view of the areas around such places as Gouda or Jerez or Chicago or Billingsgate Fish Market, one would surely see them as the centres of spiders' webs, drawing in the products and the strength of the surrounding countryside, buying cheaply from little men in order to make big men rich. Seen in this light, the Chicago stockyards or the British Factory House at Oporto or Guinness in Dublin look rather different. They are not simply old buildings, although a study of them as buildings is an important part of our equipment for understanding how traditions have grown up, and why, in some cases, they have gradually weakened and disappeared. The key question on any archaeological site is, 'What am I really looking at?'.

We can examine this more closely by relating the question to three sites, a saltworks in France, a shopping arcade in Italy and a fruit and vegetable market in England.

In the 1770s, Claude-Nicolas Ledoux, who was at that time Inspector of the Royal Saltworks in France—an important and influential post—built a saltworks on his own account, at Arc-et-Senans, thirty kilometres south of Besançon. It was a grand concept. Ledoux planned an ideal city, based on the saltworks. It was to be in the form of an enormous oval—very much like the mine workshops at Le Grand-Hornu—with the saltworks as part of the oval; the

Entrance portico to the saltworks, Arc-et-Senans.

Revolution of 1789 put a final end to the building programme; but by that time there was a grand entrance portico, a row of factory buildings, a splendid house for the director, which doubled as the administration block, and a semi-circle of warehouses and workshops. Architecturally, it was magnificent; commercially it was idiotic.

The plan was to bring brine sixteen kilometres by pipeline from a spring near the Swiss border, so that wood from the nearby Forest of Chaux could be used as fuel for the evaporating furnaces. Unfortunately, however, the brine contained only eleven grammes of salt per litre, compared with thirty-eight grammes at the saltworks on the Mediterranean coast, which used sea-water. Consequently the works was never economic to run, and it was shut down and opened up again on a number of occasions by a succession of optimists, the supply of which never seems to run out in the business world. Eventually in 1920 the Government declared the whole complex to be a national monument of the first quality and since, in France, this means that the owners have to maintain it, the company in possession at the time panicked and began to dynamite the buildings. They were eventually discouraged from going any further with this, and the State took over the premises and carefully repaired them.

If now the question is asked, 'What are we looking at?', the first and most obvious answer will probably be, 'Some elegant buildings. How extraordinary to go to all this trouble and expense, just to

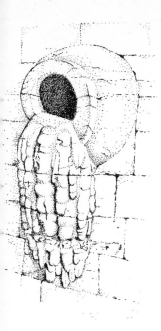

Stone replica of salt encrustation from the façade at Arc-et-Senans.

build a saltworks.' This was almost certainly the thinking of the French Government in 1920. Here, they felt, was something of architectural importance, and with a sufficiently interesting blend of grandeur and eccentricity to justify preservation. It was an art historian's decision and, in most countries, Communist and non-Communist, the majority of those who are ultimately responsible for the saving and care of historic buildings have the art historian's approach and philosophy. But in this case we are in fact studying something much more than a distinguished piece of architectural history. What is in front of us is a symbol and a product of the exceedingly civilised eighteenth-century view that useful things could and should be beautiful as well, that one had a duty to make everything as elegant as one possibly could. Clothes were not merely for keeping one warm and decent, words were not merely for communicating one's bare meaning, chairs were not merely for sitting on. One should organise the whole of one's life, even a saltworks, with style.

The saltworks is also the symbol of a man who got lost in his dreams. To construct a sixteen-kilometre pipeline nowadays is nothing, but in the 1770s it was a formidable undertaking. And to have begun it without first testing the strength of the brine was, one might say with hindsight, the act of a lunatic. But in the eighteenth century, as always, men lived by dreams and, to Ledoux, the saltworks was a beautiful idea, something for which posterity would be grateful to him. The fact that it was designed to produce salt was almost incidental.

One can hardly say that it is accidental that the Galleria Vittorio Emmanuele in Milan contains shops, since this is what it was designed for. But it gives rise, none the less, to certain interesting social questions. We can accept, to begin with, that this great shopping arcade, completed in 1865, is both an engineering and an architectural masterpiece. Its splendid iron and glass roof and its Renaissance façade make it one of Italy's most notable contributions to the glasshouse age which was ushered in by the 1851 Exhibition in London. But it is not only a technical achievement. If one stands in the middle of the Piazza del Duomo in Milan, with one's back to the west front of the Cathedral, the Galleria is on the left and straight ahead the La Scala Opera House. These three buildings, in the heart of the city, represent the three most important aspects of Italian life, religion, singing and acting, and buying and selling. To be effective as a symbol, each had to be of the highest possible quality, a cathedral in its own right, so that whatever tribulations and miseries Italy might have to endure—and there have been many during the past century—these three buildings should be always there, to remind the citizens of Milan of what Italians are capable. The fact that the shops in the Galleria are prodigiously luxurious and expensive and that few people can afford to buy what is in them is of absolutely no importance, except as a merit. If the rest of life is drab and impossibly difficult, it is encouraging and necessary to have just one or two tokens of what life was once and might be again.

It would not be right to claim a significance of quite this order for Covent Garden Market in London, but it is certainly no exaggeration to say that it was not only an inconvenient, cluttered-up fruit and vegetable market. Architecturally it is interesting, in the Victorian iron-and-glass fashion, but not as distinguished as Les Halles, the great Paris markets, which have recently been closed, pensioned off, and transferred, as Covent Garden has been, away from the central area of the city. From a town planning point of view, the Covent Garden area was a mess, but from a human point of view it was a good thing to have a market, an opera house, a publishing area and the headquarters of British Freemasonry nudging up against one another, as reminders that life has many facets and forms of expression and that there is a lot of common sense in what may look, on the surface, like an inefficient jumble.

The pure industrial archaeologist, and such creatures do unfortunately exist, is likely to see Covent Garden Market as a site to be photographed, documented and recorded before everything is demolished. He will be interested, absolutely correctly and usefully, in plans of the buildings, details of the surrounding road systems, the quantities of fruit, vegetables and flowers that were sold each day, and so on. What is less likely to be recorded by an industrial archaeologist is the old man shuffling along the pavement in search of the odd carrot or apple which is eatable, the old woman who came round every day looking for broken boxes for firewood, and the restaurant proprietor who bought his supplies here every morning and took them away with him in the boot of his car. These are the people who, like the tourists, will never be seen around now that the market has moved to its new, 'efficient' site at Nine Elms. The social context of Covent Garden was a vital part of its history, as indeed it is of Paddington Station, the docks in Boston or Krupps in Essen. Dissociated from the people and the community, industrial archaeology is meaningless and a waste of time.

Pre-1914 Covent Garden porter.

There are a number of books about industrial archaeology, but they are nearly all confined to a single country. R. A. Buchanan's Pelican, *Industrial Archaeology in Britain* (1972) is the nearest thing to a textbook yet published, and is useful for anyone who wishes to take a first look at the territory and its landmarks. It has a good bibliography. *The Archaeology of the Industrial Revolution*, by Brian Bracegirdle (1973) has splendid colour photographs, which recapture the feeling as well as the facts of these old industrial remains, and J. M. Richards' earlier book, *The Functional Tradition in Early Industrial Buildings* (1958) uses Eric de Maré's great photographic skill and sensitivity to obtain a similar effect in black and white.

Arthur Raistrick's *Industrial Archaeology: an Historical Survey* (1972) is a vigorous, freshly written book, by a man who regards the subject as one in which 'the scholar and the practical enthusiast can meet on equal terms'.

The relationship between technology and people has been explored in some detail by W. H. G. Armytage in his book, *A Social History of Engineering* (2nd edition, 1967). On the other hand, *Industry and Technology* (1963), by W. H. Chaloner and A. E. Musson, although excellently illustrated and the best book for anyone wishing to understand the broad pattern of industrial and technical development, is not greatly concerned with the people who used the machines. Terry Coleman's *The Railway Navvies* (1965, Penguin 1968) shows how the spotlight can be usefully and agreeably turned away from the engineers and financiers and on to the men who actually did the work.

The Industrial Archaeologist's Guide (1971), edited by Neil Cossons and Kenneth Hudson, covers such topics as legislation and industrial archaeology; museums and industrial archaeology; the National Record of Industrial Monuments; on-site preservation; and societies and organisations.

Britain, the United States, Belgium and the Netherlands all have active societies for industrial archaeology. The aim of the British society, the Association for Industrial Archaeology, is typical of all four. It was established 'to promote the study of Industrial Archaeology and encourage improved standards of recording, research, publication and conservation. It aims to assist and support regional and specialist survey and research groups and bodies involved in the preservation of industrial monuments, to represent the interests of industrial archaeology at a national level, to hold conferences and seminars, and to publish the results of research.'

It welcomes new members of all ages and occupations, and publishes a Bulletin six times a year. The Secretary's address is: Church Hill, Ironbridge, Telford, Shropshire, TF8 7RE.

INDEX